The Festive Soul of English Сı.˛

The Festive Soul of English Cricket

from Tunbridge Wells to Scarborough

Chris Arnot

This edition published 2019 by:
Takahe Publishing Ltd.
Registered Office:
77 Earlsdon Street, Coventry CV5 6EL

ISBN 978-1-908837-13-4

Cover image © Richard Spiller
Reproduced by permission

TAKAHE PUBLISHING LTD. 2019

To those who still love the traditions of a game played with a red ball for four or five days. Also to my beloved wife Jackie who has no great interest in cricket but still encourages me to carry on writing.

Acknowledgements

As an old hack, I'm going to mention the journalists first — more specifically the cricket writers who have stood up for the traditional form of our domestic game at a time when those running it, namely the England Wales Cricket Board, seem intent on hi-jacking high summer with ever more gimmicky intrusions. Thanks particularly to Tanya Aldred for two thought-provoking pieces in *The Observer* at the beginning and end of the 2019 season. She was rightly sceptical about the new Hundred competition that we have to look forward to next season, "edging the four-day game further to the margins". Administrators should not run a game, she pointed out, "by cutting out its heart and soul".

Thanks also to Paul Edwards for his celebrations of festivals old and new in *The Cricketer*. I met Paul at Cheltenham where he was talking on the same theme during the lunch interval while covering the Gloucestershire game against Worcestershire in his other role as cricket correspondent of *The Times*.

At this point I should mention *The Guardian's* former cricket correspondent Matthew Engel who recently wrote another celebration of festivals new and old on the paper's weekly cricket email. I've mentioned Matthew's typically witty take on Spytty Park, Newport, in more detail in the introduction to this book.

On my own travels around the country I have met so many lovers of the game that have been only too happy to talk. Too many, perhaps, to repeat all their names here. Instead I'll go from one ground to another, mentioning officials, coaches, former players, historians and some stallholders with connections to club or county.

Guildford:

Thanks to Richard Spiller, who handles communications for the Woodbridge Road ground, for the information and the pictures. Also to Guildford chairman Bob Cunningham, former club captain Tim Walter and batting stalwart Brian "Knocker" Norman for their reminiscences. Not forgetting former Gloucestershire and England wicketkeeper Jack Russell for his memories and his stall of distinctive paintings of cricketers and grounds near and far.

Arundel:

Sussex supporters Peter Styles and Tarquin Cherry proved to be genial company on the long walk from the station to the ground. And it was a privilege to meet the former Australian Test player and coach Jason Gillespie, now coach of Sussex, who was generous with his time. Thanks also to Sussex board member Jon Filby and his partner Alison Maher who was running the book stall. And to James and Doreen Birch of the Friends of Aurundel Castle Cricket Club. Finally I should mention biographer Andy Merriman who cheered me up on a damp afternoon with stories about comic characters from our youth, including Hattie Jacques and Margaret Rutherford, Tony Hancock and Sid James.

Tunbridge Wells:

Club historian David Robertson, county statistician Howard Milton, author of *Cricket Grounds of Kent*, and Richard Walsh, author of *All Over in a Day*, provided much useful background before I even set off for the Nevill Gound. Thanks also to county week co-ordinator Steve Niker and former chairman Carl Openshaw. On the day, I particularly enjoyed meeting Tony Sanders, whose excellent second-hand book stall would reappear at Cheltenham. Also John Rogers and Tim Wright, two Yorkshire supporters living in Hastings, and Michael Harvey, a Kent supporter living in Nottinghamshire. What's more, Notts batsman Chris Nash was happy to chat when I'd met him in the car park on the day before the match.

Sedbergh:

Former Lancashire chief executive Jim Cumbes had been a useful contact (as usual) when it came to explaining the county's decision to move from one of its established festival grounds, Southport, to a public-school ground in Cumbria. Thanks also to the school's director of cricket Martin Speight for information, pictures and for inviting me into the hallowed sanctuary of the members' enclosure to meet the head Dan Harrison. Lancashire supporters were full of travellers' tales about their lengthy journeys, particularly the genial Roger Sutherland. And it was a joy to hear some positive spin on festival grounds in general and this one in particular from former Lancashire and England batsman David "Bumble" Lloyd, now such an entertaining commentator on the game.

Chesterfield:

Neil Swanwick and John Windle, chairman and secretary respectively of Friends of Queen's Park Cricket, were full of helpful background information. What's more, John gave me a glimpse inside the pavilion and introduced me to dressing room attendant Edwin Clarke who had once been sent on an important mission by Shane Warne. Thanks also to Mike Taylor, chairman of Chesterfield CC. And indeed to Philip Mallon, deputy head of Old Hall Junior School, who brought a whole class of children to watch the cricket and let me talk to one or two of them.

Cheltenham:

Chris Coley, a specialist in corporate hospitality, has played a key role in co-ordinating the Cricket Week and helping to make it one of the biggest draws on the festival circuit. He was, as usual, chairing the lunchtime and teatime talks by Paul Edwards of *The Times* and *The Cricketer* (see above) and Jim Cumbes (see Sedbergh) who not only ran Lancashire CCC but played for Worcestershire in the summers and Aston Villa in the winters of his younger days. Gloucestershire historian

Roger Gibbons was full of stories of Cheltenham matches past when I eventually tracked him down in one of many tents. He also introduced me to photographer Tony Hickey who sent me plenty of images of the day. Finally, Bill Greenoff, proved to be a man of many memories, not just of Cheltenham but of any number of first-class grounds. He'd visited 55 over his cricketing lifetime.

Scarborough:

Paul Harrand, chairman of Scarborough CC, couldn't have been more helpful. He not only had an abundance of personal stories of eventful festivals past but also arranged for me to tap into Dickie Bird's memories of playing and umpiring here. Thanks to Dickie, obviously, for being as entertaining as expected. The "ladies" of the fabled tea room here deserve special thanks for the size and quality of the cakes. And it was good to share both cakes and ale with old friends Pete Dredge, now a resident of Scarborough, and Allister Craddock who had also been good company at Chesterfield. The three of us had been to some memorable Test matches at Trent Bridge. In future I suspect we may be meeting up at Scarborough almost as regularly.

Finally, thanks again to my former publisher Graham Coster, whom I've also mentioned in the introduction, for generating my enthusiasm for festivals. And indeed to my current publisher Steve Hodder whose copy-reading has been as assiduous as ever, despite having little interest in cricket.

Contents

Introduction

It was getting on for 10 years ago that I found myself Lost. Writing *Britain's Lost Cricket Grounds* was my first contribution to a lavishly illustrated series published by Aurum. Then came *Britain's Lost Breweries and Beers*, *Britain's Lost Mines* and, finally, *Britain's Lost Cricket Festivals*.

The common thread between all those books was Graham Coster. He commissioned the Lost Four and soon persuaded me that cricket festivals were something very special, very British and, what's more, they were in danger of dying out.

The facts and figures spoke for themselves. There had been sixty four festivals in 1961, an average of three per county. Forty years on and only sixteen had survived. By 2014 there were even fewer. After all, the County Championship had been split into two divisions, which meant far fewer four-day fixtures. Meanwhile, the counties had put money into upgrading their grounds and were keen to recoup their investment by staging matches at their headquarters.

Come 2019, however, and there was something of a blip in this depressing trend. It was, after all, the summer when England would be hosting the World Cup. Not to mention the Ashes. The bigger grounds would be packed with voluble crowds from around the globe. Bristol and even Taunton hosted World Cup matches, as well as every Test ground from the Riverside in Chester-le-Street to the Rose Bowl, Southampton.

And so it came to pass that Hampshire returned to the Isle of Wight for the first time since 1962 when Colin Ingleby-Mackenzie was in his prime, having led them to the county championship the previous season. Back then they crossed the Solent to play at the J. Samuel White ground at Cowes. What's more, Ingleby-Mackenzie *fell* into the Solent towards the end of a boisterous night out with Trevor Bailey, as Essex were the visitors.

Fifty seven years on and Hants took on Nottinghamshire over four days at Newclose, near Newport, built as recently as 2009 by cricket enthusiast and businessman Barry Gardener.

He died in 2015, but his son Martin and fellow trustees kept the show on the road and fulfilled his wish that the ground of his dreams should host county cricket. Apparently Newclose has a pavilion modelled on the Getty family's Wormsley paradise in the Chiltern Hills.

I say "apparently" because I didn't go. Nor did I venture to York when Yorkshire returned to their county town for the first time in nigh-on 130 years. This time they played at Clifton Park rather than Wigginton Road where Bobby Peel (see Chapter Seven) had taken nine wickets against Kent in 1890. The opposition in 2019 were Warwickshire, the county I've supported since the days of Tom Cartwright and M.J.K. Smith.

Tempting?

You bet.

But by then I was at the Nevill Ground, Tunbridge Wells, having decided to concentrate mainly on "the survivors" – the established festival grounds that have long been part of what Duncan Hamilton called "the loam and marrow" of an English summer. He happened to be writing about the College Ground, Cheltenham, an integral part of the Gloucestershire fixture list since 1872. But it could just as easily be Sussex at Arundel, Derbyshire at Chesterfield or Yorkshire at Scarborough – settings that I'd come to love for their sense of timelessness and conviviality.

With a no-deal Brexit looming, the splinters of our discontent were much in evidence all summer on the television news and in the papers. But everybody that I met on the festival circuit seemed friendly and more than happy to talk. About cricket, that is. About matches past. About watching great players close up on small grounds.

Quite a few were men of a certain age with time on their hands and many a memory. But there were women too, some engrossed by the play, some knitting or nattering while their husbands concentrated on the cricket or, in one case, spark out on a patch of grass enjoying an afternoon nap. There were younger women as well, sipping wine, prodding phones and sometimes surreptitiously eyeing the outfielder just the other side of the boundary rope. There's an intimacy about festival grounds. You feel close to the play.

You also see quite a few children once the school holidays are underway. Few watch for long. Many play impromptu matches on the grass behind the small-scale stands or rows of temporary seating. Tree stumps or dustbins double as wickets. So do the wheels of temporary toilets that have been towed in for the occasion. No matter. It's always good to see kids enjoying our national summer game.

There were two longstanding festival grounds that I'd never visited before. One was Woodbridge Road, Guildford, where Surrey had played since 1938, albeit with an unavoidable break brought about by the Second World War. The other was the aforementioned Tunbridge Wells where Kent were playing Notts in 2019. It was mid-June and the petals of the rhododendron bushes that encircle the Nevill Ground had almost faded away. But it was still a magical day in genial company with fellow spectators who'd travelled from near and far.

Kent is a big county and, like Essex and Yorkshire, the county side had been almost peripatetic at one time, travelling everywhere from Folkestone to Maidstone to Dover. And even to Blackheath as well as Beckenham in "sarf" London.

These days the vast majority of home games are played at headquarters in Canterbury. But the Tunbridge Wells Cricket Week has featured on the fixture list since 1901. As I've said in Chapter Three, the ground had been laid out three years earlier on land owned by William Nevill, who just happened to be the Marquis of Abergavenny.

One thing that it shares with Abergavenny in Monmouthshire is that both clubs had their pavilions burnt down by suffragettes in 1913.

As I recall, the Welsh ground was overlooked by the Sugar Loaf Mountain, from the top of which it must have looked like a kidney-shaped swimming pool. The boundary rope went in and out here and there to accommodate the local bowls club and the gardens of long-suffering local residents.

Mind you, fewer sixes will have come flying into their roof tiles and greenhouses since Glamorgan stopped visiting after 2007. Ten years previously Steve James had scored a century in each innings for the county side against Northamptonshire while the rain bucketed down on the other side of the mountain. Graeme Hick and Viv Richards had also made hay on those short boundaries. Asked what he thought of the ground at Abergavenny, Sir Vivian once drawled, "It isn't exactly Lord's, man, but it's full of runs and the setting's good enough to be in the Caribbean."

Full of runs?

Andrew Symonds may well have shared that sentiment. He once clouted no fewer than 16 sixes there while playing for Gloucestershire in 1995 – a world record at the time (England World Cup captain Eoin Morgan has since surpassed it).

There must be something about cricket in Wales that encourages cricketers to let rip. Those of us of a certain age will always remember the incomparable Gary Sobers hitting six sixes in one over for Nottinghamshire at Swansea in 1968.

I found myself doing a book-signing at the St Helen's ground in Swansea a few years ago. And I enjoyed it. Plenty of good stories about that Sobers over from spectators who claimed to have been there at the time. More book sales then I expected too. Which, I suppose, is a round-about way of apologising to Glamorgan supporters for the lack of Welsh grounds in this book.

You could argue that the clue's in part of the title: *The Festive Soul of English Cricket*. But then Glamorgan have been part of the English County Championship for nearly a century.

All I can say is that I've done this book with limited time on a limited budget. One day I might make it to watch a county match at Colwyn Bay, which is 180 miles from Glamorgan's headquarters at Sophia Gardens, Cardiff, and a hell of a lot further from where I live. Mind you, I've been to Newport, Monmouthshire, a fair few times and a county match was staged there for the first time for many a year in mid-May, 2019.

The game against Gloucestershire was drawn. And there was no rain, on the first day at least, according to *The Guardian's* distinguished former cricket correspondent. Matthew Engel still makes welcome, if occasional, appearances on the sports pages and on the paper's website.

So was Spytty pretty?

"From the right angle," he wrote, "it looked quite attractive. The trick was to sit with your back to the pylons, the wind turbines, the football floodlights and what one local thought was a fabrication plant."

Still, Matthew went on to point out that "Newport have become a major force in club cricket and the county were hugely impressed by the ground, the parking and — what's vital on these occasions — the enthusiasm of their hosts".

Well, I've always been impressed by Trent Bridge. Along with good friends, I've witnessed many a memorable Test match there. I've also had some memorable interviews with the splendidly eccentric, bow-tied librarian Peter Wynne-Thomas at his book-packed and newspaper-strewn lair deep in the bowels of the ground.

Earlier in the summer it was Peter who told me about Nottinghamshire's plans for a rare venture away from the Bridge. For a "home" match, that is. By chance they seem to have been mentioned fairly regularly as the away side in this book, from the Isle of Wight to Scarborough via Tunbridge Wells.

The last time Notts had played a County Championship match at an outground of their own was in 2004. And that was at Cleethorpes. In Lincolnshire, if you please. At least they'd be within their own county borders in 2019 when they were due to take on Hampshire between June 9 and 12. At Sookholme.

No, I'd never heard of it either. "Somewhere between Warsop and Shirebook," according to Peter, who went on to tell me, "It has indoor nets, a good pitch and masses of room for parking."

The ground is normally home to Welbeck Cricket Club — no longer Welbeck Colliery CC, as the pit that employed 1,400 men at its peak closed in 2010. A few former miners still play in the fourth team, I was told. One is now 64.

John Fretwell, who set up this ground and made it fit for county cricket, is now 70. "He loves his cricket and once played for Welbeck alongside miners," I was told by his brother-in-law Mark Waterfield of the John Fretwell Sporting Complex that also hosts weddings, conferences and children's parties on the site.

John himself is the son of a lorry driver who became a barber's apprentice on leaving school. He then moved into selling watches and, eventually, much else. He set up JTF Wholesale which was sold on to a venture capitalist in 2004. Two years later the footings for the new ground were laid.

The businessman who had set up another cricket-ground dream in the middle of nowhere must have been bitterly disappointed when the county's four-day first-team finally came a calling. So would Notts and England fast bowler Jake Ball who grew up playing at Welbeck.

Introduction

Why disappointed?

Because the game that so many people had put so much effort into bringing about was largely washed out by rain.

That's cricket in England for you. Never predictable.

It also rained at Arundel where I found myself for the second day of Sussex versus Gloucestershire around the same date. But at least we had a full morning's play and an entertaining day, as you can read in Chapter Two.

In Chapter Four you can read about the only occasion that I veered away from the established festival fixtures to visit a "new" county outground in a new county. New to first-class cricket, that is.

Not that there was anything new about Sedbergh School. It was founded almost 500 years ago in what is now Cumbria, except in cricketing circles. The county side is known as Cumberland and plays in the Minor Counties league.

Lancashire, on the other hand, was a founder member of the County Championship. So why did they choose to play Durham a very long way from Old Trafford in the Cumbrian Fells?

All is explained in Chapter Four. I also explain why it was worth it to take a very long train journey to the station billed as "The Gateway to the Lake District" and back again on the same day. Plus a thirteen-mile return coach journey through admittedly stunning countryside in the company of some weary and wary Lancashire supporters.

As you may have gathered, this book is by no means just about cricket. It's about the journeys I've made, the people I've met, the conversations that I've overheard and the places around the festival grounds. Particularly the pubs.

I just hope that you enjoy reading it half as much as I've enjoyed the travelling, the research and the writing.

Riveted by the afternoon's play at Guildford

Chapter One

Woodbridge Road, Guildford

Surrey v Somerset, day one, Monday June 3

It was not long after 11 am in what might be termed the refreshment tent and I could have sworn that I just heard somebody calling for "a pint of tea". Not from the pinafored women, or "ladies" as they're known in cricketing circles, serving coffees and cakes. No, this was from the bar to the right where a few festive elbow-benders were already savouring the first of the day. "T.E.A.," it transpired, stood for Traditional English Ale. So traditional indeed that it was being served straight from a barrel recently delivered by Hog's Back Brewery from nearby Farnham. Several brews from elsewhere in Surrey were similarly casked and ready to spill into glasses at the twitch of a tap.

For me it was a little early in the day for a pint. I was still trying to take in the uncompromisingly modern pavilion at the far end of the ground. There was something almost Scandinavian about the broad, flat-roofed exterior. It wouldn't have surprised me to learn that inside it was bedecked by furnishings from Ikea.

This striking addition to the Woodbridge Road ground opened in 2018, 80 years after the pavilion that it replaced. "The new one is far bigger and has better facilities," I was assured by Richard Spiller, former sports editor of the *Surrey Advertiser*, who handles "communications" for Guildford CC. "The old one looked quainter but it was falling apart. It was also a strange example of how to use space badly."

County players didn't have such high expectations of facilities back in 1938 when Surrey ventured out from The Oval to play their first match at Guildford. It just happened to be their 150th game against Hampshire and the "home" side went on to win it by an innings and 71 runs.

Surrey returned the following year, only to lose to Derbyshire by an innings and 43 runs. The match was all over by four o'clock on the second day. And soon county cricket was all over too. Not just at Guildford but all over the country. The Second World War had stopped play. Some club games continued at Woodbridge Road, however. Local lads who would become nationally known as "the Bedser twins", Alec and Eric, made an early appearance here. So did George Edwards – or Sir George, as he later became. The aircraft designer's knowledge of the intricacies of leg spin was said to have been useful in helping Barnes Wallis develop the bouncing bomb.

County cricket resumed in 1946 and Surrey duly reported for duty in Guildford in late July. Alec Bedser bowled throughout the first innings, having taken 11 wickets the previous day in his maiden Test match at Lord's against India. This time he took a mere five for 21 and Surrey went on to win by nine wickets. Once again Hampshire were the victims.

Seventy three years on and there were quite a few Hampshire supporters here for the first day of Surrey v Somerset. "I live at Alton," Ian Powell told me. "But it's easier to get here by public transport than it is to the Rose Bowl."

These days it's known as the Hampshire Bowl -- or the Ageas Bowl after its major sponsor, an insurance company. Opened in 2001, the ground is renowned for being closer to the M27 than the middle of Southampton. It was due to host India v South Africa in the World Cup in two days' time and no doubt it would be awash with flag-waving fans, weather permitting. But for a four-day county match it would be largely empty, rather like The Oval where spectators might need megaphones to converse with a stranger.

What Ian and other Hampshire and, indeed, Surrey supporters like about outgrounds such as Guildford is their intimacy. Spectators were huddled together on rows of portable chairs and the players were close by. Woodbridge Road itself is a busy dual carriageway. Buses and lorries

12

thundering by are protected from flying cricket balls by a very high fence. There's a railway bridge spanning the four lanes, just past what's known as the railway end of the ground. So, yes, you could also hear trains pulling into the nearby station. But, no, the noise of passing traffic on rail and road couldn't suppress the leisurely sense of stepping outside the daily grind.

As I stepped out from the refreshment tent, a green swathe of land known as The Mount surged up to the right of the new pavilion, somewhere beyond deep long-off. Over cover-point, meanwhile, the tower of the cathedral was clearly visible through the branches of one of many trees that dwarfed the advertising hoardings and indeed the scoreboard. From the back of the seats on the far side, I could just about make out that Somerset were 35 for three. Former Guildford lad Rikki Clarke was bowling from one end while 6ft 5 South African Morne Morkel was striding in from the other.

Enter George Bartlett, only to be dropped by Clarke at slip off his first ball. An expensive miss as it turned out. Bartlett would go on to make the highest score of his career.

But that was still a long way off. For now it was just after 12 and clouds were eclipsing the morning sunshine. Still, the light was good enough for play to continue and I settled down for a while near the pavilion end, having been texted by my former publisher Graham Coster. As I said in the introduction, it was Graham who commissioned me to write *Britain's Lost Cricket Grounds* for Aurum. Among others. And the others included *Britain's Lost Cricket Festivals*. Visiting the survivors in places such as Cheltenham, Chesterfield and Scarborough had ignited my love of these occasions when the counties came to town.

I was sitting between Graham and an immaculately spoken Somerset supporter who introduced himself as Charles before turning to the man behind and enquiring with impeccable politeness, "Is my hat obscuring your view?" On being told that it was, Charles delved in his bag and came up with something flatter. He seemed to have a fair selection of headgear in there as well as an enormous pair of field glasses that were capable of spotting sparrows on distant horizons let alone studying deviations in pitch and turn out in the middle.

Eventually he put them back in the bag and pulled out a scarf emblazoned with the name and logo of Torino Football Club. "I once worked in a garden centre just outside Turin and used to go to watch them play," he told me by way of explanation.

At this point I noticed the only red-topped tent among the white marquees encircling the ground. Former England wicketkeeper Jack Russell was evidently in town, as he tends to be when there's a chance to sell some of his evocative paintings to cricket lovers.

I'd first met him five or six years previously at the Cheltenham College ground where his former county, Gloucestershire, were entertaining Kent on a glorious day in high summer. The fierce sun had lit up the buttressed frontage of the neo-Gothic chapel. Next door was the twin-towered gymnasium which turns itself into the pavilion at festival time. "Like a dungeon with showers," was how Jack described the changing rooms. "When you turn the lights off, it's pitch dark. Beautiful place to have a kip."

So what did he think of the new pavilion here at Guildford with its upgraded facilities?

"The old one was good enough in my day," he shrugged. "But then I grew up getting changed in sheds."

An original Jack Russell could set you back a few grand. But there were plenty of prints on sale here for anything from £35 to £250. Most were of matches at grounds such as The Oval, Taunton and, yes, Guildford. But there were other pictures as well. Here a combined harvester in a setting that suggested somewhere in the Cotswolds; there a train passing by on the Severn Valley Railway.

Standing between Jack's stall and a marquee full of venerable Surrey Committee members in blazers and panamas was a character that I'd been introduced to earlier. Former Guildford batting stalwart Brian "Knocker" Norman was about to turn 80. Not that you'd know it by the way he had just stooped effortlessly from his considerable height to pick up and throw back a ball that Bartlett had clouted over the rope at long-on. Somerset had added another 30 without loss and their number five had evidently "got his eye in". By county standards the boundaries here are not too far from the wicket but, according to Knocker, "it doesn't seem that small when you're out in the middle. Mind you, I played at The Oval once in a cup competition and that put it in perspective."

At which point I remembered an earlier conversation with Guildford's cricket chairman Bob Cunningham who was recalling Surrey players returning from The Oval at festival time. "Last year we had Jade Dernbach, Rikki Clarke, Ollie Pope and Will Jacks – all former Guildford lads," he'd told me with some pride. "They like coming back, I think, and feel at home here."

Former club captain Tim Walter, now 55, had then reminisced about the days when he'd led such distinguished cricketing figures as the Bicknell brothers (Martin and Darren) and Ashley Giles MBE, a key figure in the unforgettable Ashes series of 2005 and, more recently, England's director of cricket. "We had a very good coach at that time," Tim had recalled, "Brian Ruby was influential in pushing talent through Guildford. The Bicknells are still linked with the club. But Martin now runs cricket at Charterhouse while Darren's up in Nottingham, so neither is likely to be here today, unfortunately."

At least there was still Knocker who was now reminiscing about the days of his youth. Woodbridge Road had seemed like Shangri-La when the stars of Surrey's famous '50s side breezed into town. "I couldn't afford to come in for county matches," he recalled, "so I peered through the fence and tried to catch a glimpse of the Bedser twins and Peter May."

Ah yes, Peter May – or PBH May as he was titled in the days when "gentlemen" cricketers had initials in front of their surnames to distinguish them from mere "players" from the lower orders. A former Charterhouse and Cambridge toff he May may have been, but he just happened to be one of the most stylish English batsmen of my childhood. Peter May's Book of Cricket was one of my treasured possessions.

Walking back towards the refreshment tent as the lunch interval approached, I noticed a man in shorts and sandals sporting long black socks and cradling a book by one Peter May. A very different Peter May as it turned out. This was a fat paperback by the Scottish novelist and screenwriter whose details come up now if you Google the name.

Needless to say, the area around the bar was considerably more crowded at one o'clock than it had been just after 11. There was apparently going to be a beer festival between the end of the Somerset game and the arrival of Yorkshire.

Not that there was a shortage of choice today for the first part of a two-match cricket festival. After due consideration, I settled on two pints from the Crafty Brewery, based on a farm in a wood at Dunsfold some 10 miles away. The Crafty One turned out to be a straw-coloured pale ale with a good hoppy finish. It went well with a couple of egg mayonnaise sandwiches that Graham had just queued for at the nearby tea bar where the home-made lemon-drizzle and the coffee and walnut were disappearing fast. Washed down by pints of T.E.A. more often than not.

Cakes and ale, eh?

Not for me, thanks. I'd wait until the players went off for tea in the fervent hope that a slither of coffee and walnut might survive the next two and a half hours.

Hopefully we'd survive too, bearing in mind that I'd caught my first train at some ungodly hour this morning and someone in the bar had warned me that this was "not a place to fall asleep in the afternoon". Big-hitters had tended to make the most of short-ish boundaries at festivals past. Gordon Greenidge had made a double century here for Hampshire in 1977. And the following year Mike Procter had rattled up 154 in under two hours for Gloucestershire, including eight sixes.

In 1982 Surrey captain Roger Knight's car had taken a direct hit as Surrey and Glamorgan piled up nearly 1,400 runs between them. "Several nearby houses lost some tiles and slates," according to George Plumptre's book Homes of Cricket.

More recently, Kevin Pietersen warmed up a chilly Woodbridge Road by making 234 not out from 190 balls, including eight sixes, in 2012. According to Wisden, it was Surrey's highest individual score at Guildford, surpassing local boy Darren Bicknell's 228 not out against Nottinghamshire in 1995.

But the highest score of all here was 342 in 2006 by Justin Langer. Not for Australia but for Somerset. On that occasion the visitors declared on 688 for 8, only to be surpassed by Surrey's 717. Result: match drawn.

Were we in for a repeat in 2019?

Not if the early part of the afternoon session was anything to go by. Tom Banton, who had shared a partnership of 95 with Bartlett, had gone 24 balls without scoring when he edged Matt Dunn to gully for 44.

By now we were sitting square of the wicket in the front row. At least the reassuringly towering figure of Morne Morkel was patrolling the square-leg boundary. Surely he was capable of catching any six hooked in our direction.

One or two spectators had indeed nodded off in the torpor of mid-afternoon, including a woman not far from us who was lying face down on the grass, her broad-brimmed hat strategically balanced on the back of her head. Either she had supped too well of the red wine that her other half was still savouring or she was bored rigid.

Nearby a Japanese lady was gazing inscrutably at the afternoon's play while sitting on a cushion from Wimbledon and occasionally reaching for a box of Lindt chocolates that her husband was cradling.

Graham, meanwhile, was prodding his phone to check the score in the England World Cup match at Trent Bridge. Pakistan had made 348 for eight in their 50 overs. Here, meanwhile, Somerset were 146 for four with Bartlett on 59. It was 2.45 and the sun had finally emerged from behind the clouds to spill gold on the tops of the hitherto white marquees.

Had he been here to commentate, Henry Blofeld would have been wildly excited at this point. A wagtail had fluttered down to join the pigeons pecking around in the outfield. They were close to where a young couple were sprawled on the grass just this side of the rope, arms around each other's shoulders but eyes firmly focused on play.

Well, it's always good to see young people at this, the time-honoured form of the game – a game that is played in fewer and fewer state schools and largely confined to satellite television. It was noticeable that the main party of uniformed children here today were from Lanesborough School where fees are around £5,000 per term.

Back on the field, meanwhile, Bartlett had just opened his shoulders to deposit a six just beyond the stand named after S1 Capital, "official stockbroking partners of Guildford CC". That was followed by an effortlessly contemptuous square cut for four off Clarke. It was around 20 minutes to four and he'd just reached 93. Evidently looking for a "ton" before tea.

One of the pleasures of cricket festivals is that spectators are allowed to wander on to the pitch during lunch and tea intervals. You can stroll right up to the wicket and pontificate sagely about the likelihood that it has to offer bounce or turn. But don't you dare step on it. Oh dear me, no. One of the senior stewards from The Oval had come to see that rule enforced. Not that he needed to. We kept our distance. "It's a bit different from yesterday," he confided, referring to Bangladesh's victory over South Africa. "Lovely people, the Bangladeshis, but they get very excited." Understandably so. Such a result would have been unthinkable not so long ago.

By the time I made it back to the refreshment tent, there was not a crumb of coffee and walnut left. Nor a lemon drizzle. I settled for a raspberry ripple cake which, one of the delightful ladies behind the till confessed had had to be "bought in from Marks and Spencer". Ah well, there are worse things in life, I suppose.

As I emerged clutching two teas and a cake, members of the Surrey County Cricket Dining Club had finally risen after a lengthy lunch in the marquee next door. One was sporting a startling pink-striped jacket as he and a few fellow diners sauntered off to join the hoi-polloi. At which point Bartlett clouted another six. Nowhere near the diners, luckily. Putting down one's wine glass and putting up one's hands to take a catch might have been a tiresome distraction. With spillage, what's more.

Somerset's number five was finally caught [Ben] Foakes bowled Morkel for 137 and the visitors themselves were all out for 344. Not bad for a side that had at one point been 33 for five. By now some of their more bucolic supporters were in full voice – not least a character known down in Taunton as The Tractor.

I'd first spotted him by the bar much earlier in the day, sporting a straw hat and a t-shirt emblazoned with the name of his website: tractordriver.co.uk. Now, as the Surrey openers faced two tricky overs from Craig Overton at one end and Jack Brooks from the other, The Tractor was revving up. "Come on, Jacko," he bawled throughout one over. "Come on Brookerrrrr," he roared throughout the second. To no avail as it turned out. Surrey survived on 0 for 0 to fight another day.

For Graham and me it was time for the second pint of the day en route to the station, at the pub we'd spotted a hundred yards or so up the other wide of the Woodbridge Road. No, it wasn't called The Cricketers. For some reason it went under the title of The Drummond and the walls inside were decorated with pictures of Ronald Colman rather than Peter May, the Bedser twins, Tony Lock or Jim Laker.

Ronald Colman? He was in his prime long before my time. "But one of his films was Bulldog Drummond," Graham recalled. Made in 1929, apparently. At least that explained the name if nothing else.

We called for two pints of T.E.A. and took them out into the garden to catch the dying embers of the sun at the end of a memorable first day of what promised to be a memorably festive summer.

Three days later Somerset beat Surrey by 103 runs.

Surrey v Somerset

*Gazing at the more scenic side of Guildford, away from
the busy Woodbridge Road*

Woodbridge Road looking idyllic, despite nearby traffic and trains

Pictures by Richard Spiller

The very modern pavilion that looks as though it might be internally furnished by Ikea

Boundary fielders always seem close to the spectators at festival grounds

Pictures by Richard Spiller

Chapter Two

Arundel Castle

Sussex v Gloucestershire, day two, Wednesday June 12

The raucous squawkers of a seaside-town dawn chorus had finally quietened down. Either Brighton's greedy seagulls had discovered a bag of cold chips in an alleyway or the remains of a gourmet meal on a patio.

Bliss. We could finally go back to sleep.

Then it started. The rain was soon hammering down on the skylight window at our daughter's house. Not so blissful after all. Rain did not bode well for events ahead.

The previous day had been a significant birthday for my wife and the weather had duly obliged. Sun had beamed down. It had been bright too for the first day of the cricket festival in nearby Arundel. I was due to be there later this morning and the weather had changed, changed utterly. An incredible beauty was shorn of its potential for a good day out. By that I mean that Arundel Castle provides the setting for one of the most attractive cricket grounds on earth and, having enjoyed a few festivals past, I'd been looking forward to watching Sussex take on Gloucestershire.

The Brighton branch of the family harbours a computerised know-all called Alexa. She can turn off lights, switch on television channels of choice and is an endless source of information. "Alexa," one of our grandsons drawled drowsily, his mouth full of breakfast cereal, "what's the weather going to be like today in Arundel?"

The impeccably spoken Alexa duly responded with the weather in Aberdeen.

He tried again and this time she came up with the right place but the wrong answer – as far as I was concerned anyway. It was due to rain for much of the day. There was, though, a glimmer of hope for the morning's play.

So off I set on a train journey of around 23 miles that took the best part of an hour and a half, involving two changes.

First stop: Hove where Sussex play most of their fixtures at a ground packed with history and a character captured with witty insightfulness by Michael Simkins in his books *Fatty Blatter* and *The Last Flannelled Fool*. Second stop: Barnham, eventually.

The train trundled along, offering occasional glimpses of the sea between the backs of boarding houses or industrial estates. In a rare departure from habit, I'd bought the *Daily Telegraph* earlier in the vague hope that this most conservative (as well as Conservative) of newspapers might offer more coverage of county cricket than *The Guardian* or the *i* paper.

Well, there was plenty of cricket on pages two, three four and five of the sports section. First up was a spread about the drug culture apparently prevalent at the highest levels of the game. Then a harrowing interview with former England batsman Robin Smith on how his alcoholism and depression had led to him planning his suicide.

A round-up of action from the previous day's county matches was squeezed into five paragraphs at the bottom of page 13, below extensive coverage of cycling and opposite in-depth golf analysis. In paragraph three came news that Sussex opener Will Beer had scored a career-best 76 not out at Arundel as Sussex reached 257 for five at stumps. And . . . er, that was it.

On Barnham Station I met a man sporting a white shirt under a smart blazer and a Gloucestershire Exiles tie. It was hardly a surprise to learn that he'd been travelling for considerably longer than I had. "Set off at

6.15 this morning," he confided after ordering "one of those new-fangled coffees with bubbles on". The barista looked temporarily baffled before tentatively suggesting, "A latte?"

"Ay, that's it," said the Gloucestershire exile before going on to tell me, "I'll have to leave early to catch the first train back at 10 past five, which means that I might be home by about 10.30 tonight. That's dedication for you."

Suitably impressed, I wandered along the platform to where two much younger men stood studying a film of something or other on a phone. One of them had a cricket sweater tied around his expansive girth. Yes, Peter Styles still played the game. Only last Sunday he'd hit a brisk 43 for Brunswick Village CC, not far from his home in Brighton. His day job was as head of public relations for a property company, but he always took the week off for the Arundel festival. So did his mate Tarquin Cherry, project manager for a software company. "My colleagues are somewhat baffled as to why I'd want to spend four days sitting in a field," he smiled as we boarded the final train. "I've told them that when I die I want my ashes scattered over the pitch at Arundel."

Hopefully that will be a long way in the future. Certainly the Castle ground is a long walk from the station here on the outskirts of town. Still, Peter and Tarquin proved lively company as we set off at a brisk pace along footpaths strewn with the blooms of mid-June leaning through adjoining fences. They may have been weighed down by heavy drops from earlier downpours but, for now at least, it was dry, albeit a little on the grey side.

The skyline ahead was dominated by the turrets and battlements of the castle itself. Across the bridge over the River Arun we went and up the steep main street, past tea shops, book shops, antique shops and art shops. Not forgetting the "artisan bread" and "local cheese shop". Oh, yes and a half-timbered post office. Almost next door to the imposing 19th century Catholic cathedral was the St Mary's Gate Inn and opposite – at last – the entrance to the Castle ground.

Nearly there.

But not quite.

Discreet little signs with the single word CRICKET were pinned to ancient fences and lamp posts as we strode on along one path and another, past stables and outbuildings a-plenty.

Was the walk worth it?

You bet it was. Even on a grey and cloudy day the setting still looked sublime once we finally clapped eyes on it. What's more play was underway. "The game's afoot," as Henry V might have put it through his spokesman William Shakespeare were this Agincourt rather than Arundel.

Beer had advanced to 83 from his overnight score. Added seven more runs in other words as he moved with due care towards what he and Sussex supporters hoped would be his maiden century. His partner David Wiese, meanwhile, had come in at number seven with the evident intent of getting on with it. He'd just clouted a six over one of the hospitality tents. Tarquin beamed happily. "We were only 47 for two at lunch yesterday," he mused as we eased ourselves into a row of empty portable chairs. "It was the slowest scoring rate I'd ever seen," he added, as one who'd grown up in the post-Boycott era.

Wiese's six had rolled off down a distant bank. Meanwhile, Peter was clambering up the bank behind us for his first pint of the day. Unlike Guildford, the choice here was simple. You could have Harvey's, Harvey's or Harvey's. That would suit me come lunchtime. Harvey's Best, from the venerable brewery in nearby Lewes, had been a flavour to savour ever since I first sampled it at my son-in-law's local while playing pool with my eldest grandson. Yes, I can still get down with the kids.

For now, though, it was time to get up and grab a word with Jason Gillespie who had just strolled past in his track suit. A distinguished test player for Australia for 10 years, he was now coaching at Sussex. I held my voice recorder aloft as he gazed down from his imposing 6ft 5 and recalled the two occasions that he'd played here. "Once was for Yorkshire, back in 2006. Think I got a 'four-for'." (You did, Jason: four for 89 in Sussex's first innings. There wasn't a second innings for them, however, as they didn't need one. The home side won by an innings and 25 runs.)

"Bowling here was a bit hard on your legs as it's quite a soft ground," he went on. "What a setting, though. The lads loved coming here." Even the Australian "lads" who were used to much harder pitches. Jason also recalled playing here in a "tour opener" against the Duke of Norfolk's XI back in 1997. "Can't remember too much about the game, though." Well, for the record, Mr Gillespie, you took four for 21 and you Aussies won a 50-over match in mid-May by 113 runs.

It was the 15th Duke of Norfolk who had the ground laid out over 3.5 acres in 1895. Exactly 80 years later his daughter-in-law, Lavinia, formed the Friends of Arundel Castle Cricket Club after the death of her husband, Bernard, who had put on matches for players from all levels of the sport.

Touring sides have long made a habit of calling in to grace the ground with their presence and warm up for the season ahead. In the year 2000 Zimbabwe played a West Indian side in which Sherwin Campbell, Shivnarine Chanderpaul and one Brian Lara all scored centuries.

The Sussex first XI came here initially in 1972 for a limited-overs match in the John Player League. Gloucestershire were the visitors on that occasion as well. What's more, they won by two wickets, largely thanks to the great all-rounder Mike Procter who took five of them for just 10 runs. (I like to think that John Arlott would have been in the commentary box on that occasion, his incomparable claret-honed tones a marked contrast with the clipped diction of Jim Laker.)

Sussex played their first County Championship match here in 1990. Hampshire were the visitors. Chris Smith scored a century for them; Colin Wells did the same for Sussex. Result: match drawn.

An extraordinary game in 2012 saw Sussex scrape home against Durham by two wickets, despite making only 94 for 8 in their second innings. The first innings had been even-Steven with both sides amassing 231. "On a pitch offering pronounced seam movement throughout and uneven bounce later in the game, neither set of batsmen covered themselves in glory," as Wisden reported after Durham had "surrendered any momentum in the third afternoon" by reaching 38 for six. They were finally all out for 93, Paul Collingwood stemming the flow of wickets for a while with a gritty 29. Having finished with match figures of nine for 50, the Australian Steve Magoffin then saw Sussex over the line by hitting their top score of 23.

High points for the "home" side here include Murray Goodwin's 235 against Yorkshire in the game that Jason Gillespie recalled from 2006.

And the low points?

Well, they were bowled out by Worcestershire for just 71 in 1997. And two years later they let Leicestershire build the biggest score ever seen in a first-class match at Arundel, eventually declaring on 566 for eight.

Nonetheless, Sussex board member Jon Filby assured me that "everybody loves it here". That includes visiting supporters such as the Exiles tie-sporter that I'd met on Barnham Station. "I should think there must be a good 200 Gloucestershire supporters here today," Jon surmised. "And they come because it's such a beautiful place to watch cricket. In the sun yesterday I reckon we had a crowd of over 3,000."

One of the ground's many attractions remained the view over the Sussex Downs from The Gap, as it has always been known, between trees and what looked like the ruins of an old chapel. Members of the crowd tended to gather there at lunchtimes on fine days, pints of

Harvey's in hand, contentment spreading across faces as rural England unveiled itself in all its summer finery.

Ironically, considering its visibility all over town, there didn't seem to be a view of the Castle from within the Castle ground with its Castle End. All those trees in full summer bloom were obscuring it. "You can see it in the winter months," Jon assured me.

We were chatting by the book stall run by his partner Alison Maher. Indeed he's just bought her a book on Sunderland football legend Len Shackleton from another nearby stall run by the Friends (of Arundel Castle Cricket Club, that is). But why Shackleton? Admittedly he also played Minor-Counties cricket for Northumberland but somehow I doubt that he ever came as far south as Arundel.

"I did," Alison explained. "Come this far south from Sunderland, I mean," she added in an accent that bore little trace of Wearside. "Well, I went to university in London and I've lived down here for quite a long time."

Her stall stood close to the red-topped tent where former Gloucestershire and England wicketkeeper Jack Russell was once again ensconced with his paintings. "We always do well here," Jack had told me as we'd met up for the first time since Guildford all of nine days ago. As for Alison, she'd sold many a cricket book in the previous day's sunshine. "We had six tables out yesterday," she said wistfully. Today there were a few biographies for sale and many more in plastic containers. An all-too-imminent downpour could wreak havoc, even on hardbacks. One of those containers harboured an impressive collection of Wisden's, some dating back to the 1930s. The name Wally Hammond would have featured prominently as one of the greatest English batsmen of his or any other day.

By chance there was another Hammond out there on the field of play today. Miles Hammond (no relation) was due to open the batting for Gloucestershire. Would there be a repeat of the century that he'd scored at the Cheltenham festival the previous year on only his fourth first-class appearance?

We'd have to wait a while to find out. Beer and Wiese were building a useful partnership for Sussex who were 321 for five some 10 minutes after midday. Wiese had provided most of the entertainment. He'd just hit Chad Sayers and David Payne for straight sixes. Quite a few fours as well, one of which had thumped into the scoreboard close to where I was now perusing a load of old balls.

The Friends were offering these battered spheres of worn leather bound by faded seams for three quid a time. "But we are open to negotiations on that," I was told by the Doreen Birch, a Sussex member for many years with her husband James. There were panama hats and miniature bats on sale as well. Books, too. And bottles of wine? "They're part of the raffle prizes," Doreen informed me.

Proceeds go towards "youngsters less fortunate than us", as James confided when I bought a strip of tickets later on. Arundel has an indoor cricket school, paid for by the late multi-millionaire philanthropist Sir Paul Getty and formally opened by the Prince of Wales in 1991. Nearly 30 years on and it still hosts youngsters from inner-city London to give them coaching sessions as well as trips around parts of rural and coastal England that they could never have imagined. "We took one party to Littlehampton," James went on, "and one of them asked me 'what's that'? He was pointing at the sea. Never seen it before."

I didn't witness Wiese's dismissal for 67 – lbw, apparently, to a quicker ball from left-arm spinner Graeme van Buuren. But I was walking between the scoreboard and the members' enclosure when I looked up to see one of Payne's seamers pin back Beer's off stump. Cue groans from Sussex supporters and hearty cheers from the Gloucestershire contingent. He was on 97, three short of that elusive century, and he'd been out there for seven hours and 41 minutes. A kindly steward allowed me to hang about near the ancient trees beneath which many members were gathered, now wearily rising to their feet to applaud as Beer trudged back to the pavilion.

Cricket can be a cruel game.

At least the rain held off until lunchtime, by which time Van Buuren had picked up his third wicket by bowling Chris Jordan for seven. Sussex were 351 for eight. There'd been no play at Worcester or Leicester and the Kent game at Canterbury had been abandoned. Or so the public address system proclaimed. Mind you, there had been some cricket at Taunton where the Australia were 281 for five in their World Cup match against Pakistan.

The damp afternoon here at Arundel could have been depressing as well as frustrating. But I'd seen off a smoked salmon sandwich from the Tea Hut with a pint of Harvey's from the Brewery Bar. Now I was sitting under a wooden shelter enjoying a splendid slice of salted caramel cake while chatting to the aptly named Andy Merriman about Hattie Jacques and Margaret Rutherford. He'd written biographies of both those formidable matrons, among others.

Turned out that Andy's father was Eric Merriman who had penned the scripts for Beyond Our Ken, a comedy show on the old BBC Light Programme — half an hour of fun that lightened the load of those interminably tedious Sundays of the late 1950s and early '60s "when I were a lad" (as they rarely say in Arundel).

On an adjoining table sat a woman grappling with the *Telegraph* crossword under a huge blue and white umbrella. Her other half, meanwhile, was prodding his phone for news from Taunton. A few tables away sat a woman in a dog collar. Whether she was from the Catholic cathedral or the 14th century parish church across the road I didn't bother enquiring. Nor did I ask her to send up a prayer for the sun to come out. Her God, Catholic or Protestant, may well have had more pressing issues to deal with.

The umpires strolled out at 2.40 during an apparent drying up of the drizzle. Shortly after their return to the pavilion, however, came an announcement that there would be a further pitch inspection at 3.30 with a view to "restart play at four".

Needless to say, it didn't. The clouds were still heavy when we decided – rightly, as it turned out – that that was it for the day. So we mooched off down the lengthy tracks into the town.

It took a while to locate the entrance to the castle, opposite the remains of the Blackfriars Dominican Priory. Closing time was about half an hour away. In the circumstances, it wasn't worth shelling out the entrance fee of £22.

By now the sun was hardly going down behind the yardarm. After all there was no sun. But it was approaching 5pm and, just across the river from the boat yard and tea rooms, stood the White Hart. Again the only draught ale was from Lewes ("the guest beer will be delivered tomorrow") and again I wasn't complaining. A pint of Harvey's Best in a fine Harvey's pub with decorative Harvey's mirrors: what more could a man want? Especially as Andy was now regaling us with tales about not just Jacques but also her husband John le Mesurier as well as Tony Hancock, Sid James and Barbara Windsor.

On the scrubbed tables and wooden settles either side of the central fireplace were parties of festival-goers who, despite losing half a day's play, now seemed to be embroiled in enjoyably boisterous conversations. Like us, they must surely have concluded that the White Hart was a top spot to stop for rest and refreshment on the lengthy trek back to Arundel Station.

Unless, that is, you had to catch the 5.10 on a much lengthier trek to Gloucestershire.

Two days later the match was drawn. Five sessions had been interrupted by rain.

Arundel Castle

The Castle Ground Arundel on a much sunnier day

View of the Sussex Downs from "The Gap"

Pictures by Graham Coster

Chapter Three

The Nevill Ground, Tunbridge Wells

Kent v Nottinghamshire, day one, June 17

The forecast had been good. The sun was out. The rhododendrons were not, however. Admittedly a hint of pink peeped through the bushes and trees here and there. But, by and large, they'd been and gone.

Had this been late May or early June they would have been in full bloom, encircling the Nevill Ground with a glorious swathe of colour. That grandee of cricket writing and commentary, E.W. Swanton, used to gaze fondly at them over his gin and tonic, once describing Tunbridge Wells as "no mean contender for the most delectable English cricket ground".

Even largely petal-less, it looked a picture for cricket-lovers lucky enough to be here on a sunny Monday. Some spectators had already moved their portable chairs into the shade of one or another of the many mature trees and bushes as Jake Ball came on for Nottinghamshire with Kent already 13 for one. Ball was soon steaming in from what's known as the Railway End, although the railway is nowhere near as close as it is at Guildford. I knew that, having walked here from the hotel where I'd been staying for a long weekend with my wife. After leaving her at the station to meet an old friend from Hastings, I'd joined the steady file of festival-goers striding from station to ground via a long, paved passageway between high hedges.

"You're in for a treat," I'd been assured by Eddie Allcorf, a Kent supporter since 1979. "It's atmospheric, timeless and there's a real-ale tent. What's not to like?"

Surprisingly, Jack Russell wasn't flogging his paintings here, as he had been at Guildford and Arundel. No doubt I'd bump into him at Cheltenham, somewhere near the book stall run by Tony Sanders. "Cheltenham's very strong for sales, and so is this place," Tony told me. "If I could only do two festivals for the rest of my life, they would be the ones," he added as potential customers browsed through books on everyone from Fred Spofforth, the "demon" Australian fast bowler of the 1870s, to David Gower, the elegant English batsman of the 1980s. Gower made a characteristically graceful 115 at the Nevill Ground in 1981. For Leicestershire, as it happened, although he was born in Tunbridge Wells.

Tony, it transpired, lived just over the border in East Sussex. "I used to love it when the two counties played each other at the end of May with the bushes in bloom," he sighed.

It's said that the boundary between Kent and Sussex used to follow the course of a stream that ran beneath the Nevill Ground. But that was in the early 20th century when county matches here were still in their infancy. Even now it may be only a slight exaggeration to ponder the possibility of someone hitting a six into the next county.

Maybe Chris Nash tried it when he made his one-day debut for Sussex at Tunbridge Wells in 2005. "I was on 40 or so when Min Patel got me out," he'd mused when I'd met him the previous day. (I'd been taking sneaky preview of one of the few surviving festival grounds that I'd never clapped eyes on.)

Nash is now tied up with Notts. Quite by chance I'd bumped into him in the car park as he lugged his gear towards the pavilion. He seemed quite happy to stop for a chat adjacent to an ancient public phone box that looked as though it might have been one of Gilbert Scott's early designs. "I've always enjoyed playing here," Chris reflected. "Trent Bridge is a classical cricket ground but, with 2,000 people in a place with a capacity to hold more than 10 times that number, it can feel empty. Come to outgrounds such as this and it feels far more vibrant with 2,000 spectators."

"Surely the wicket wouldn't be as good as Trent Bridge," I suggested. "Or Canterbury."

"Well, I've played three championship games here and the wickets have always been fine — even if they do give a bit to the bowler."

He'd still have been playing for Sussex in the summer of 2017, unaware perhaps of the chaotic build-up to the match here at the end of May. The wicket wasn't seen as fit for county cricket. Nor, indeed, was the outfield. By that time care of the ground had long been in the hands of Tunbridge Wells Borough Council. "The groundsman had left the local authority which then appointed a park-keeper to look after preparations," David Robertson, honorary curator for Kent CCC, had told me from his home in Sandwich. "The club had to step in with support from its full-time ground staff at Canterbury."

They must have performed something of a pre-match miracle because the game went ahead as planned at the Nevill Ground with Kent scoring 369 in their first innings, 298 for two in their second and beating Sussex (164 and 356) by 147 runs. A positive run-fest compared to the days when uncovered wickets were part of the game rather than the fault of the local park keeper.

On June 15th, 1960, Kent scored 187 here before bowling out Worcestershire for 25 in the first innings and 61 in the second. Kent's David Halford took four for seven in the first innings and five for 20 in the second. Worcestershire's Ron Headley, otherwise known as "the black Bradman" got a "pair".

"Cowdrey was terribly embarrassed," I'd been told by Richard Walsh, author of a booklet called *All Over in A Day*. Yes, it was supposed to be a three-day match, as county games were in those days. And, yes, the Cowdrey in question was Colin of that ilk, captain of Kent and, like his England contemporary Peter May, another unlikely boyhood hero of mine.

Why unlikely?

Well, I'd always leaned towards supporting the Players rather than the Gentlemen in their annual matches, until those daft distinctions between amateur and professional were finally ditched in the early '60s.

Cowdrey was very much a "gent". He cut a somewhat portly figure, yet he could time a shot or pouch a slip-catch with seemingly effortless ease. "Sir" Colin, as he later became, joined the pantheon by scoring his hundredth 100 in 1973 at Mote Park, Maidstone, one of many out-grounds that Kent no longer play on.

"There have been 43 of them since 1709 when there was a match against Surrey at Dartford Brent," according to county statistician Howard Milton, author of Cricket Grounds of Kent. "They still play at Beckenham as well as Canterbury, but the match at Tunbridge Wells is the only one that feels very much like a festival."

The Nevill Ground staged its first county match in 1901, having opened three years earlier on land then owned by William Nevill, the Marquess of Abergavenny. His family's estate had long been at Eridge Park, just south of the town. Tunbridge Wells, that is, not Abergavenny. Don't ask me to go into why nobility named after a town in Monmouthshire should end up in Kent. You might as well ask why the Dukes of Norfolk have long been based at Arundel Castle. It's complicated.

There is, however, another connection between Tunbridge Wells, this prosperous borough in the south-east of England, and the place that bills itself as the "Gateway to Wales". Both had cricket pavilions that were set fire to by the suffragettes in 1913. The one nestling serenely in the shadow of the Sugar Loaf Mountain, where Glamorgan used to be regular visitors, was only partially damaged. But the one that had been designed for the Nevill Ground by one C.H. Strange was completely destroyed. With it went the archives of the Bluemantle Cricket Club. Mind you, there is now a Bluemantle Stand, built in 1995 close to the "new" pavilion. (It offered elevated views of the 2019 festival match, albeit only for those prepared to fork out an extra fiver.)

Had the destruction of the original pavilion been fiction rather than fact, Sir Arthur Conan Doyle would have set Sherlock Holmes the task of truffling out the "female hooligans", as the author called the suffragettes who'd set the place ablaze. Sir Arthur had a house at nearby Crowborough and had played for Tunbridge Wells. It seems that he was only too willing to speak out at a meeting in the town called by the National League for Opposing Women's Suffrage. Setting fire to the pavilion, he maintained, was the equivalent of "blowing up a blind man and his dog".

The building that replaced the original has a reassuringly traditional look about it, based as it was on the original design. A series of concerts at the Tunbridge Wells Opera House came up with the dosh in double-quick time and the "new" pavilion was up and ready for the 1913 Cricket Week.

Certainly the lay-out of pavilion's upper reaches keeps the scorer busy. The clock fronting the large central gable splits the scoreboard. Total, wickets and batsmen's scores are on one side, other details such as bowlers and last man's score on the other.

Whoever was up there for the first day of the Nottinghamshire match was moving between the two at regular intervals. Wickets were falling fast in the early stages.

I had an ideal view of one of them, standing as I was (very still) by the side of the sightscreen at the Railway End when Luke Fletcher clean-bowled Heino Kuhn for nine. "Well done, Luke," shouted one of two men from Trent-side borough of West Bridgford whom I'd been chatting to at the time. The other was notably silent at that point. Chris Walker, I'd noticed, was sporting a "Kent Legends" t-shirt under his jacket. Yet, like his friend Martyn Shaw, he worked for Nottinghamshire County Council, just across the road from Trent Bridge, where he spent many a summer's day watching Notts play.

"I was born and brought up down here," Chris explained. "Once played third-team cricket on this ground. I was 26 when I moved up to Nottingham, and that was in 1982." Neither he nor Martyn would have

39

preferred to have been at Welbeck Cricket Club's ground where Notts had ventured to play Hampshire the previous week – the first time they'd left Trent Bridge since they played at Cleethorpe (Lincolnshire) in the early Noughties. The Welbeck match had been ruined by rain. "A pity," Martyn shrugged. "They have a very good cake stall at Welbeck. I think Jake Ball's mum's involved."

Ah yes, the "ladies" and their cakes. "Where would cricket be without them?" I pondered as I wandered back towards the book stall while recalling the coffee and walnut in the Ladies' Pavilion at Worcester. My reverie was interrupted at this point by a group of kids enjoying an impromptu cricket match with a tennis ball in one of the open spaces between the bushes and the backs of the temporary seating. Some were of Asian and West Indian heritage, I noticed. All were playing happily together. Heartening to see for one such as me. Well, I have lived most of my life in places much more multi-cultural than Tunbridge Wells.

"I see they'd elected a new Pope," somebody observed drily as smoke started to rise from a nearby chimney. More of a funnel, really, and it was attached to the nearby pizza stall. Lunch wasn't too far away. Zac Crawley had just passed his 50 and Kent their hundred, albeit for four.

Make that five. Ollie Robinson had just been caught in the slips by Ben Duckett off a mean ball from Ball. For nine, as it happened. That seemed to be the standard score for the Kent middle-order today.

Wine was flowing freely in a hospitality tent occupied by Charles Stanley, "wealth managers". Lunch there would be somewhat more exotic, one imagined, than the pork scratchings being munched, or rather crunched, by a man sporting an extraordinary hat topped by a clump of red feathers. Around the brim was a band proclaiming him to be a supporter of Kent County Cricket Club. Yet it transpired that Michael Harvey lived in Kimberley, Nottinghamshire, and had travelled down with two staunch Notts supporters.

"My Dad was from Dover and my Mum from Sandwich," he said by way of explanation. "We were a Coal Board family and we moved to the Nottingham area in the 1960s. Via the Black Country, as it happened."

At least that explained the scratchings, very much the pièce de résistance in the pubs of Tipton and Brierley Hill. Something of a gastronomic rarity in Tunbridge Wells, I would have thought. Surely Michael hadn't acquired them at the stall where you could have anything you like, be it bacon, tuna or "organic" steak and chips, as long as it was covered with cheese. Not just any old cheese but Raclette cheese, if you please. Very popular with the Swiss and in Savoie in the French Alps, I'm told. Tunbridge Wells, too, judging by the queue that was beginning to form.

As it happened, I finished up eating cheese, albeit a straightforward Stilton sandwich in the beer tent on the other side of the ground. It was a little early for a glass of port, the accompaniment favoured by Stilton aficionados, so I called for a pint of Wantsum IPA. A wise choice, as it turned out. It's not often that a beer down here in the deep south keeps its head, especially when it has come straight from the barrel. The brewery is at St Nicholas in Wade, also in Kent, albeit some 58 miles from here in the far east of this expansive county.

Others in the tent were cooling their fevered tongues with this and other ales, having ordered the dish of the day – chilli ferried from the kitchen by a poor woman who had evidently spent a hot morning slaving over a hot stove. She brightened considerably when somebody told her, "You do the best chilli in Tunbridge Wells."

I wanted some more Wantsum but decided against it, for the time being at least. In the gents at the back of the tent, I found myself reflecting not for the first time, on the improved sanitary provision since the more bucolic days of cricket festivals. Hot water, liquid soap and paper towels were all available.

But what was this?

There were women looking at us while we peed. Very attractive young women, I might add, with mouths agape as they gazed down from the wall above the urinal. Photographed models, needless to say, and in the festive spirit of the occasion they raised a smile if nothing else. Until, that it, I noticed that I was standing under a blonde peering through a magnifying glass.

Time to send a letter to the *Daily Telegraph*, perhaps, signed by one "Disgusted of Tunbridge Wells".

Or perhaps not.

Instead I re-joined a small party that I'd met earlier and who were now ensconced in a row of seats to the left of the beer tent. Like our friend Lauri, who was lunching with my wife somewhere in The Pantiles, they hailed from Hastings. At least that's where they lived.

John Rogers was quite evidently a Yorkshireman. "Late on in life, I've met a young lady who's 17 years younger than me," he confided. "Her twin sister has a holiday home in Hastings. We went down there at weekends, fell in love with the place and moved there."

At this point I reminded him that Yorkshire were playing Warwickshire today. In York, what's more. That historic and characterful county town was being graced by a visit from the county side for the first time since June, 1890. "Wouldn't you rather be there, John?" I suggested.

He leaned back for a moment and soaked up the sun as another wicket fell and Kent had slumped to 119 for six. Eventually he responded. "I wouldn't mind being in the members' tent here in Tunbridge Wells with a chilled Chardonnay," he said. "But when all's said and done, I'm here anyway with good friends from Hastings. And one of them supports Yorkshire. That'll do me."

The other Yorkshire supporter was to my right. "I support them," said Tim Wright, "because of family connections." He'd been born just within the county borders some 67 years ago – a necessary pre-requisite to play for the county in those days. If he was good enough, mind you. And if his family hadn't moved south. "Scarborough is still one of my favourite grounds," he smiled fondly.

At least Scarborough still has a cricket festival (see Chapter Seven). Indeed Yorkshire still play there more than once a season. Sussex haven't been to Priory Meadow, Hastings, since 1989. The ground harbouring what W.G. Grace once described as "the truest piece of turf in all England" is now a bog-standard shopping centre called . . . well, Priory Meadow.

I'd caught a glimpse of ground in the '90s shortly before the bulldozers had moved in. A splendid setting, to be sure, surrounded as it was by elegant boarding houses clambering up the cliffs towards the castle with the sea nearby. "Yes, I remember it well," Tim reflected. "In fact, I played there back in the day for Hastings and St Leonard's Priory. It was one of my favourite grounds. Along with Scarborough, of course."

Of course.

For now, though it was time to sit back and relish the pleasure of being at the Tunbridge Wells festival on a sunny afternoon in-mid June. Out in the middle, Kent were staging something of a comeback. A six had just disappeared over the sightscreen and into the bushes beyond. Zac Crawley was approaching his century.

He would eventually make 111, a major contribution towards his side's 309 all out. At one point it had seemed quite possible that they wouldn't make 200, let alone 300-plus. Nottinghamshire would be 30 for no wicket by close of play. Not that I would see them bat, having been conscious that we were on a pre-booked train to London. First I had to walk back to the town centre, catch a bus up the hill to pick up our case from the hotel overlooking the rock-strewn Common near the summit of the aptly named Mount Ephraim. Oh yes, and pick up my wife.

By now the "ladies", as they say in cricketing circles, were relaxing in the Opera House. Yes, the same Opera House where money to rebuild the burnt-out pavilion had been raised a century or so ago. No, they weren't watching La traviata. They were sipping white wine in a building that had retained so many of its original Edwardian features, inside and out.

It's now a branch of Wetherspoon's.

Suddenly it seemed a long time since 5.15 when I'd been standing outside the beer tent at the Nevill Ground savouring a pint of Shepherd Neame Master Brew, served in a proper glass "glass", while chatting to a chap who'd grown up in Tottenham at a time when I'd worked on the local paper there.

Now that really was a long time ago. But while we're strolling down Memory Lane, I might as well go back to a period 10 years before I found myself on the mean streets around Tottenham High Road and White Hart Lane. My parents had taken me to Tunbridge Wells where the streets were not mean. Anything but. The Georgian colonnade known as the Pantiles appeared positively exotic, even though many of the residents seemed somewhat staid. I remember being taken for afternoon tea in a café where "entertainment" was provided by a decrepit trio in faded dinner jackets sawing away at violins. Even my Mum was trying to stifle her giggles. For me, about to enter my teens in what would become the "swinging sixties", it was embarrassingly ludicrous.

Well over half a century on and Tunbridge Wells has shed its dated image as a haven of blimpish ex-colonels and matronly, fur-stoled wives and widows. Its pubs and coffee bars are full of 'cool' young people who probably regarded me as antiquated if, hopefully, not quite so ludicrous as the Pantiles Trio.

But the town remains a bastion of architectural elegance built around green spaces galore. The Nevill Ground is just one of them. Long may its rhododendrons flourish – long enough, hopefully, to coincide with next year's cricket festival.

* Three days later Kent beat Nottinghamshire by 285 runs.

The view from the beer tent

A Gilbert Scott original? The phone box in the car park

The pavilion with the clock dividing the scoreboard

Michael Harvey, who lives in Notts but all too evidently supports Kent

Chapter Four

Sedbergh School

Lancashire v Durham, day two, Monday July 1

By the time we reached Oxenholme, "Gateway to the Lake District", I'd heard the recorded messages from Virgin Trains so many times that I can still recite every station stop on the way to this day. In order, what's more, from Birmingham International to Lancaster. It beats counting sheep as a way of getting to sleep. And talking of sheep, I'd seen more than enough of them once we'd moved into Cumbria.

Yes, Cumbria. Lancashire CCC had chosen to play a county match beyond its own county borders for the first time, to the disgruntlement of some of its supporters. When the train finally pulled in to Oxenholme, via "Wolverhampton, Crewe, Warrington, Wigan North Western, Preston" and so on, I joined a queue in the underpass for one of the shuttle buses laid on by the club's officials from their headquarters at Old Trafford, Manchester.

Quite a bonus for me, as it happened. I'd expected to have to shell out for a taxi to cover the final 13 miles, in which case my eyes would have been fixed on the fare meter rather than the Cumbrian countryside beyond the window.

Behind me in the queue were two men from Accrington and, it's fair to say, they were not happy Stanleys. "It's ludicrous," grumbled the one sporting a claret-and-blue Burnley FC shirt under his windcheater. "We've had to get a train to Preston, then this one. Now we've got a long bus journey."

"Is it easier to get to Old Trafford?" I enquired innocently.

"Oh, yes," they chorused.

"But surely it's going to be a lot prettier at Sedbergh. Quite a setting to watch cricket, I'm told."

Accrington Burnley shrugged. "I've never been there before and I couldn't come yesterday because the trains were not compatible with the match times on a Sunday."

At this point there was an intervention from Roger Sutherland, a comparatively genial gent whom I'd met up with on the platform a few minutes earlier. "It is a lovely place to watch cricket," he confirmed "I met somebody here yesterday who, like me, had come from Wigan on the train. 'It would be really nice to be here," he said, 'for an away match.'"

Roger then went on to reveal that a coach full of Lancashire members had been driven all the way from Manchester the previous day, only to discover that the vehicle was too large to fit into the narrow streets of Sedbergh. Rather than just let them get off, the driver had taken them on a lengthy tour of the area in the hope, presumably, of finding another way in. At one point, apparently, they'd found themselves back on the M6.

At least the shuttle bus that we eventually clambered aboard looked small enough for a small town to accommodate. I found myself sitting next to a man of few words who was bent over the weather map in his *Daily Mail*. "This place we're going to," he muttered, "is within the boundaries of the Yorkshire Dales." He shook his head ruefully, as it to confirm his worst forebodings.

It wasn't long before a brown road sign appeared on one of the many winding lanes that we tootled along. "Western Dales" were the words I could just about made out through a rain-swept window. Everybody else stared steadfastly ahead. The windscreen wipers were on. So were the headlights of the few vehicles that made up the oncoming traffic in this idyllic if somewhat isolated neck of the woods.

Just about everyone on the bus was wearing something waterproof. From bitter experience they knew that you don't go to a cricket match "oop 'ere" without being suitably clad. As the old saying about Old Trafford goes, if you can see the Pennines it's going to rain and if you can't see them it's already raining.

Like an idiot, I'd left home at the crack of dawn and mistaken the blue skies above as the sign of a fine day to come. Accordingly, I was sporting nothing more than a lightweight jacket over my shirt. I'd even put some suntan cream in my knapsack.

It wasn't as though I didn't know the north-west. As a long-time freelance writer, I'd travelled everywhere from Warrington to Morecambe Bay and beyond. I'd even been a student at Lancaster University more years ago than I cared to remember.

The sense of weary fortitude that had pervaded the shuttle-bus seemed to evaporate once we'd parked up, climbed down and set off at a brisk pace along a main street.

"Oh, there's a chip shop," Accrington Burnley acknowledged. He seemed to be brightening already at the prospect of visiting The Haddock Paddock at some point. Mind you, "truly authentic fish and chips" were also available from one of the food stalls inside the low-ish wall of local stone that encircled the school grounds. Or you could sample "haggis cooked in a crispy batter with chips" as well as other delights. Across the way was another stall offering, in a perhaps unconscious echo of Arnold Wesker, "Chips with Everything". You could have chips with cheese, chips with curry, chips with gravy.

Fees at Sedbergh School, founded in 1525 and sometimes known as "the Eton of the North", amount to over £8,000 a term (or over £11,000 for boarders) but some effort had evidently been made to appeal to the tastes of the lower orders.

Then again, the stalls may have been brought here at the behest of Lancashire. Club and school had been liaising since the previous year. "Paul Allott [Lancashire's director of cricket] had been up to watch a game here," head teacher Dan Harrison told me in the official hospitality enclosure, once my wrist had been encircled by one of those plastic bands bestowing exclusivity. "I showed him around and he was evidently impressed by the facilities," the head went on. "We met up again when he invited me to a Twenty20 Roses match at Old Trafford."

The atmosphere in Manchester must have been somewhat more raucous than it was today, one imagines. But a deal was evidently sealed. After all, Old Trafford would be hosting World Cup matches as well as an Ashes Test in 2019. Another outground would be required. Admittedly the county side would make its regular visit to Aigburth in Liverpool. But not to Southport, a ground that I remembered visiting for a county match and a book-signing a few years previously. Enjoyed it, too, despite having had to catch three trains there and three trains back on a busy Saturday when the football and rugby league seasons were already underway.

Before I'd set off for Sedbergh, former Lancashire chief executive Jim Cumbes had told me that he had been "a great supporter" of Southport "simply because they were so enthusiastic and really worked so very hard to put games on. However, they were hampered by a small ground, a sometimes dodgy wicket, and poor dressing-room facilities."

The imposing school pavilion to our left, with its balcony and inbuilt scoreboard, was evidently good enough inside to satisfy Allott and other Lancashire officials. As for the wicket, groundsman Martin South had come to Sedbergh via the Bradford League. Ay, Bradford's "over 't' top" in Yorkshire. But outside Test and county cricket, there are few more demandingly competitive players and officials.

"Some of the Lancashire ground staff came up to have a look at our pitch and they didn't seem to have any complaints," I'd been told by the school's Director of Cricket, Martin Speight. "For the past 10 or 12 years we've played against the Lancashire Academy – good games on good wickets."

Cumberland have also played Minor Counties matches here as well, maintaining the name bestowed on the county long before the local government reforms of 1974. Since then large parts of Lancashire have been subsumed by Greater Manchester. So maybe there was some logic in staging a game on a ground more accessible to residents of the northern part of one county as well as the southern part of another. "We do have a Lancaster postcode," I'd been assured by Martin, a man who wears more than one hat (or cap). He also teaches classics and art. Oh yes, and he was once wicketkeeper-batsman for Sussex CCC. And Durham, indeed. So who would he be supporting today?

"I'm not telling you."

Out in the middle the covers were being removed. It wasn't too long after 11 and the clouds that had draped themselves over the summits of the surrounding hills, or "fells", had begun to lift and drift. As the Durham players skipped down the lengthy flight of stone steps from the pavilion, they appeared to be dwarfed by Winder Fell at the far end of the ground. So was everything else, including the tower of the parish church of St Andrew's nestling in the lower slopes.

Winder boasts by no means the highest peak in these parts but, by heaven, it provided a spectacular backdrop for a game of county cricket. No wonder Paul Allott had described this place as "one of the most picturesque grounds in the UK".

Later in the day I would have the privilege of seeing one of the world's great fast bowlers running in with Winder beyond. Jimmy Anderson would surpass yet another wicket-taking milestone. But that was a while away yet. For now I just felt glad to say that at least we had play. Lancashire were about to resume on their overnight first-innings total of 275 for 5.

Looking on between the hospitality area and one of two packed stands stood three staunch Lancastrians clutching pints of Black Sheep. A good sound bitter, as I recalled. Not that I was thinking of trying one just yet. "It's from Yorkshire," said one of the trio, bitterly. "And it's cost us the best part of a fiver each. I wouldn't mind but we're

51

Lancashire members and we have season tickets. This is supposed to be a home game but we've had to pay to get in."

"Only eight quid for people of a certain age," I reminded him, having decided to play devil's advocate. "Wasn't it worth it for a setting like this?" I added as the sun briefly broke through on cue.

He was having none of it. Obviously took pride in playing Mr Grumpy, as the smirks on the faces of his mates confirmed. It turned out that he came from Warrington which, come to think of it, has been part of Cheshire since '74. I thought better of mentioning that. Instead I tried to wind up the Warrington Whinger by finding good things to say about Yorkshire. "Michael Vaughan was a shrewd captain in that unforgettable Ashes series of 2005," I reminded him.

"That's because he was born in Lancashire." He almost smiled and his mates almost chortled, confirming that this was very much his party piece. A bit of an act, in other words.

At this point I spotted a familiar face and heard his familiar voice. David "Bumble" Lloyd had provided rich entertainment over the years with bat or microphone in hand, for Lancashire and England, Test Match Special and the Sky commentary box.

He seemed happy to talk to me once I'd briefly detached him from a gathering near the sightscreen. "I'm a big advocate of festivals from my playing days," he confided. "We used to go to Leyton and Ilford, Tunbridge Wells and Cheltenham, and it was great. Wonderful atmosphere. On the way here today, we came past loads of fields and then queued up behind two chaps carrying their own chairs. That's what festivals are about."

Even when it meant crossing county borders to stage one?

"I'm not bothered. When I was coaching at Old Trafford, there were occasions when it felt that we were a bit too insular, serving only Manchester and the parts around it. Here we're not far from the north of the county and a stone's throw from Kendal. It's a mere detail."

It transpired that Bumble had driven here this morning from Yorkshire. "We've got a holiday cottage there and I live there most of the time. My wife still works at Lancashire, but she comes over when she finishes. We also have a house in Cheshire."

Here in Cumbria, Lancashire were 313 for nine by 12.30. Former England bowler Graeme Onions had just been caught Ned Eckersley bowled Nathan Rimmington for a duck. Enter one J.M. Anderson, bat in hand. Ten minutes later, Jimmy was heading back up those steep stone steps again as a short, sharp shower had set in. A good opportunity, perhaps, to take a look at the lunchtime offers. Not the battered haggis and chips, thanks all the same. Instead I set off on a short stroll to the school's Queen's Hall, the exterior of which was bedecked with abundantly colourful hanging baskets.

Inside there was a sign pointing to the bar upstairs, for "Lancashire members only". Downstairs it was a case of "all welcome". Sausage rolls, herb or pork chorizo, were available for £2 and either cottage pie or chilli for £7.50. You could have either with sticky toffee pudding "plus extra toffee sauce" for a tenner all in.

There was no Lancashire hot pot on the savoury menu, I noted. But according to a man from Preston sporting a Lancashire sun hat, "the beef stew and dumplings were delicious yesterday".

Behind him a television screen was, somewhat jerkily, transmitting the match live. The rain shower had evidently been a short one. Lancashire had advanced to 328 for nine. Never mind sausage rolls or cottage pie. It was time to get back to the action.

Anderson was out for four just after one o'clock, leaving Josh Bohannon undefeated on 33 and Lancashire 337 all out. Lunch had been put back to 1.30 to make up for time lost to rain. Nobody seemed to have told the man on the heavy roller, however. As batsmen as well as bowlers took to the field, he rolled on for a while. When he finally rolled off, the droll soul on the public address system called for "a nice round of applause for the roller man".

The openers, Cameron Bancroft and Alex Lees, had the tricky task of facing Anderson and Onions under leaden skies while jet planes from a nearby RAF station roared by. The sun had long gone and, apart from the jets, there was a bit of a nip in the air. Slip fielders thrust their hands in their pockets between balls, as it were. But no catches came their way and the "visitors" were nine for no wicket by 1.30.

As they trudged back up the pavilion steps, I took the opportunity to head out of the ground in the direction of a stone-fronted building which I'd been eyeing for some time.

The Red Lion offered a decent pint of Wainwright's golden ale. Eventually. Two young lads were on duty, one behind the bar and another in the kitchen, as the cricket crowd piled in. I gave up on the idea of ordering food, found the only available stool at the far end of the bar and settled for a packet of crisps.

Brewed on this side of the Pennines, the beer cost a mere £3.60. Somewhat surreally, Bob Dylan singing *Like a Rolling Stone* was emanating from a speaker somewhere below the low, beamed ceiling. Not that you could hear much of it above the clatter of cutlery and the chatter of festival-goers discussing the morning's play.

Having seen off the Wainwright's and crunched the last crisp, it was time to hit the town. Well, have a quick look at Sedbergh without missing too much of the afternoon session.

There was nowhere near enough time to do justice to a place that claims to sell more books per head of population than anywhere in the UK. Not only were its meandering streets well stocked with book shops, there were also books available in cafes, tea rooms and even The Haddock Paddock. A redundant stone-lined bus shelter harboured four shelves of hardbacks and paperbacks that could be borrowed and returned at your leisure. Needless to say, it had been re-christened the Book Shelter.

Would that I'd had more time to browse. Instead I had to head back towards the ground, via Yorkshire Dales Antiques and a sweet shop reminiscent of my childhood. Jars in the window were stuffed with humbugs, barley sugars and much more.

Round the corner and across the road, St Andrew's Church looked much bigger, needless to say, than it looked when viewed in the context of Winder Fell from the other end of the cricket ground. Parts of it dated back to the 12th century, but the windows were of similar vintage to the school – not far off their 500th birthday.

At the bottom end of the graveyard was a footpath with a signpost to the cattle market. It was lined with stone-wallers – people leaning on the wall watching the cricket, in other words. I thought about telling the Warrington Whinger that he could have seen the game for free from here, albeit without beer (even Yorkshire beer). Or food for that matter.

Talking of which, I was feeling a little peckish. Yes, I'd only had a packet of crisps and, no, I hadn't dabbled with any humbugs or barley sugars from the sweet shop.

Back at the ground I settled for a roll stuffed with hot pork from a nearby farm. With stuffing and apple sauce, what's more. Just the job, even though I'd declined the crackling as a potential threat to the back fillings.

Finding a seat on which to eat was not easy. Eventually I squeezed on to the end of a row towards the rear of one of those packed temporary stands. The sun had reappeared over one or another of the surrounding fells and the scene was set for a memorable afternoon.

Durham were doing well. Until, that is, Alex Lees was caught by Anderson off Mahmood to break up an opening partnership of 70.

Cameron Bancroft was at the other end. Would he, one of the infamous "sandpaper trio", be in the Australian side for the Ashes series due to start at Edgbaston the following month?

(Yes, was the short answer to that, as it turned out.) Certainly he'd faced Anderson on much bigger grounds than Sedbergh's. Watching them resume their confrontation in such an intimate and picturesque setting was something to savour. Once, that is, I'd followed up the pork "batch", as we call them where I come from, with an "artisan" ice cream from another local farm. What was it about being in the open air for the day that made you so hungry?

Come the tea interval and school pupils were standing outside the Queen's Hall advertising the availability of scones with jam and cream inside. Not for me, thanks. Couldn't eat another thing.

Instead I let my rum-and-raisin cone settle while watching a very young boy wielding his mini-bat quite stylishly as his ever-patient dad tossed up endless deliveries. To me it's always a pleasure to see kids playing cricket with enthusiasm. Not long afterwards it was even more of a pleasure to witness Anderson nip one back off the seam to bowl Bancroft for 77.

But the most significant moment was still to come. In the following over, the man who already has an "end" named after him at Old Trafford trapped Graham Clark lbw for a duck. It was Anderson's 950th wicket. Glad I managed to see it. Sorry I had to rush off soon afterwards to catch the 5.30 shuttle-bus in order to connect with my pre-booked train.

Typically, the best weather of the day was upon us by then. It seemed positively tropical on the southbound platform on Oxenholme Station. By the standards of north-west England, that is. Morecambe Bay would have looked a picture. So would the inland lakes and fells. But I was heading in the other direction, "calling at Lancaster, Preston, Wigan North-Western, Warrington . . . "

Several hours later I made it home and two days later the match was drawn, with Durham on 194 for six.

The imposing pavilion at Sedbergh School

Lancashire folk well wrapped up for a day in the Cumbrian fells

Pictures by Martin Speight

The view from St Andrew's Church

The Red Lion pub, handily placed for the lunch interval

Chapter Five

Queen's Park, Chesterfield

Derbyshire v Northamptonshire, day three, Tuesday July 16

It was close. Very close. No, I don't mean the result of the above fixture. I mean my initial decision to come on the first day. That would have been Sunday July 14, which just happened to be the date of the World Cup Final. Much as I love watching cricket at Chesterfield, I'd decided to postpone my visit. That would give me chance to watch England and New Zealand on the telly with one of my grandsons who just happened to enjoy playing cricket before England's triumph in the most extraordinary finish to a final that any of us could have imagined.

The Monday would have been a good day to be at Queen's Park — fine weather, plenty of wickets and the ground abuzz on a day when cricket had dominated the front pages and even made the lead story on BBC national news bulletins. Alas, it also happened to be a day when I had an unavoidable meeting.

Tuesday it was then. Still good weather. Trains on time. Met up at Chesterfield Station with Allister Craddock, former producer of the Politics Show on East Midlands BBC and a good mate since our long-ago days on Radio Nottingham. Allister had been at Trent Bridge the previous day to see Nottinghamshire lose to Surrey within three days.

Neighbouring Derbyshire were about to do the same against Northants, it seemed. They had five wickets left and were still some way short of their second innings target of 319 to win.

There was no time to lose. Up the hill from the station we went, over the bridge, past the weathered stones in the graveyard surrounding the crooked spire of St Mary's and All Saints, 228-ft high and 9ft 5 inches off its true centre. We turned left at the Rutland pub with its frontage turreted, as though ready to repel an invasion across the nearby border with Yorkshire.

The narrow passageways of The Shambles suddenly opened out into that marvel of a market place, its many stalls open to the skies but not to the public. Not today anyway, being a Tuesday. Just as well perhaps. We had no time to dawdle. On down the sloping slabs we strode until the imposing Portland stone pillars of the town hall's grandiose 1930s frontage loomed into view to our right. Nearly there. Once, that is, the narrow passageway across the road had given way to the broad bridge spanning a four-lane highway and the River Hipper.

And there it was at last: Queen's Park in all its glory. To the right were the tracks of the miniature railway that circumnavigated a lake brushed by reeds and a weeping willow of impressive circumference. To the left was the children's playground in front or the café with its own "gelataria". Ice-cream parlour, in other words.

Well, it is the home of Frederick's "award-winning" ices. Founded in 1898, according to a logo on one side of two vans that were also in their usual places. One was just outside and the other just inside the ground that, by a curious coincidence, hosted its first county match in the same year. By another coincidence, Derbyshire stopped coming exactly a century later.

Thankfully, they resumed their annual visits in 2006 by which time a hefty sum had been spent on bringing the facilities up to scratch, largely thanks to part of a four and a half million pound grant bestowed on Queen's Park by the Heritage Lottery Fund. "Almost uniquely the Lottery had allowed some of the money to be used for cricket," I was told by Mike Taylor, chairman of the Chesterfield club side. "Usually there's a hard dividing line between sport and heritage. But there was a feeling that cricket was intrinsic to the park, so a lot of the money went on upgrading the pavilion."

I'd first met Mike the previous year, having come to Queen's Park on a Saturday when Chesterfield CC had been playing Rolleston. I was diligently researching a column in *The Cricketer* magazine called *County Cricket in 100 Objects*. The "object" in this case had been Puffin' Billy, a blue engine with gold adornments and a black funnel, that pulls the miniature railway around the lake at weekends and during school holidays. The driver, one Lewis Cree, had an Afro hairstyle and turned out to be a guitar technician by trade. He'd been on the road with Def Leppard, among others. When on the rails, he'd always shown due respect to the cricketers by not hooting Billy's horn when somebody was coming in to bowl.

Batsmen hadn't necessarily shown the same regard for those circumnavigating the lake. And why should they? Their job is to score runs. I'd been here for a county match a few weeks earlier when Alex Wakeley of Northants had lofted successive sixes off Hamidullah Qadri, over deep long on and out of the ground. As the ripple of applause had faded and the two men next to me had resumed their discussion about Sheffield Wednesday's chances for the following season, I'd heard a reassuring hoot from Puffin' Billy. "One or two sixes have landed in the lake," Lewis had shrugged. "But they haven't come anywhere near the train."

It is a moving target, I suppose. Which is more than can be said for those sitting outside the Frederick's "gelataria" and, indeed, their children. The playground is now closed for precautionary reasons during Twenty20 games. Not even the upwardly extended fence next to the horse chestnut tree at the park end of the ground could be guaranteed to protect the "little 'uns" from mighty smiters such as Surrey's Ali Brown who had apparently cleared the fence with three sixes in succession. Or so I'd been told by chairman Mike on that memorable Saturday afternoon of miniature train travel and club cricket. Two laps for two quid on Puffin' Billy and no charge, needless to say, to watch Chesterfield v Rolleston.

To view Derbyshire's last rites against Northants two days after the World Cup Final, 2019, cost a tenner. "I told the bloke on the gate 'it might only last three-quarters of an hour'," said a man from Matlock who was seeing off a Frederick's cornet with some relish. "He said 'it's still 10 quid to get in'."

And still worth it, I thought to myself, as we finally sat down close to the horse chestnut – though not quite close enough to benefit from its spreading shade. Those seats had already been bagged. Derbyshire were 178 for six, Tom Lace having been caught by Temba Bavuma off Brett Hutton for 41.

Another Hutton, Len of that ilk, had brought his post-war Yorkshire side here in 1946 and, after two overs, called for the pitch to be re-measured and re-set. It was found to be 24 yards long instead of the regulation 22.

Seventy three years on and the woman in front of us was knitting furiously what looked like a lengthy scarf for chillier days ahead. A few seats to her left was a younger man chatting amicably with Northamptonshire's Rob Newton who was fielding on the boundary and, seemingly, quite happy to converse between balls. That's festival cricket for you.

I've been coming to this particular festival for the past six years and the only time that I haven't enjoyed it was in 2016 when the match had been called off without a ball being bowled. Damp outfield and wet patches on the bowlers' run-ups, we were told. Eventually. News of the abandonment had not spread to those of us who had travelled here from well beyond the reach of the local media. Waste of time, waste of money, waste of breath when we came to complain to officials. Northamptonshire were the away side on that occasion as well. They seem to be Chesterfield regulars, along with Yorkshire.

The Tykes were due in town on the forthcoming Saturday for a Vitality Blast T-20 game. All 5,000 tickets had been sold in advance. For now, though, it was 11.40 on a Tuesday morning and Derbyshire had just lost another wicket. Harvey Hosein had been lbw to Luke Procter for 22.

It was time for an amble round the ground. To the right were a line of lime trees and spectators were already helping themselves from a pile of portable chairs to find a position offering shade, a decent view of the game and, in some cases, close proximity to the Brampton's Brewery tent.

My re-acquaintance with Chesterfield's fine micro-brewery would have to wait for at least 10 minutes. First I wanted to take in my annual view of the crooked spire. Yes, I know that we passed it on the way here but I've always enjoyed the sight of it seeming to peer over the trees on the far side of the ground, as if trying to check the score.

The first time I'd seen it was from just behind the members' enclosure in 2013. A man who had just drained two blackcurrant smoothies with hardly a pause for breath had pointed it out. Six years on and where had it gone? "You can't see it no more," an ancient local worthy confirmed. "Them trees on the far side have grown too tall."

As it turned out, I was offered a splendid view of the spire later on. But that was from the scorers' room at the front of the pavilion – a pleasure still to come. For now I just wanted to check that everything else was where it should be.

Yes, the tea bar was still there, between the members and the pavilion. Yes, you could still buy a slice of cake or a doughnut for 60p or a chocolate biscuit for a quid. And, yes, there was still a bar at the side of the pavilion, seemingly open to all and sundry while offering a chance to see the game from almost behind the bowler's arm.

Conscious that I had to be at the Brampton's tent shortly, I declined the offer of what looked like a decent pint. But I did happen to be in a plum position to see Matt Critchley bowled by Matt Coles for 19. By now Derbyshire were 212 for eight. Would they last until lunchtime?

No, was the short answer to that. They were nine down by 12.15 when Tony Palladino was caught behind off Procter for one. Still, at least Fynn Hudson-Prentice and Ram Rampaul were putting up some belated resistance. Balls began disappearing to the boundaries, if not into the lake or indeed through the windows of the conservatory behind the members' enclosure.

Surrounded by lawns inlaid with impeccably ordered flower beds, it no longer harboured the "purple-flowered bougainvillea and other exotic plants" that were evidently here when George Plumptre was researching his book on Homes of Cricket in the 1980s. Instead there was a selection of Derbyshire shirts, hats, bats and so on for sale inside. "Go and have a look," said one of the shop assistants who stayed outside. "It's too hot for us in there," she added. Certainly I didn't dally for too long, having decided against buying yet another seamed ball for my cricket-mad grandson who has a habit of depositing my devious off-breaks into neighbours' gardens or otherwise impenetrable bushes in the local park.

Instead I strolled back through the lime trees, reflecting on the Chesterfield festival as an engaging mixture of the grandiose and the homely. Queen's Park remained a fine formal setting, with its lake and flower beds, its conservatory and band stands, but the occasion seemed less corporate than some. The ground wasn't plastered with sponsors' names and only one hospitality tent was available for wining and dining.

For the rest of us the main food offer, apart from the cake stall, was a van offering burgers. Not any old burgers but "hand-made" burgers. Of course, there may well have been far more vans and stalls come Saturday's full house for the Vitality Blast.

"There'll be 5,000 here for that," I was told by Neil Swanwick, chairman of the Friends of Queen's Park Cricket, ensconced with a colleague at a table strewn with leaflets and handily positioned in a corner of the Brampton's tent.

The Chesterfield festival date had been decreed before that of the World Cup Final, I'd been told. So how many were here on Sunday?

"Obviously it was a lower crowd than normal for the first day of a Derbyshire match here, but there were still around 300. Yesterday there were 2,000 plus and there was a superb atmosphere with lots of wickets falling. We have a visitor who comes from Scotland every year, a couple from London and this season we've had someone from Perth in Australia."

Was he here for the Ashes?

"No, he was planning to go back before the series starts, apparently. He just liked coming to smaller grounds like this one."

Perhaps an even more surprising revelation was that someone from Yorkshire had joined the Friends. "He said he'd rather be here than at Headingley," Neil added before going on to emphasise that he didn't want the festival to become simply a magnet for people of a certain age. "We're really interested in promoting cricket for kids. Already we have a sort of third-eleven tournament with mixture of 11 and 12-year-olds and some over-40s. But we're also running coaching courses for youngsters so that we can be as inclusive as possible."

As if on cue, a primary school party appeared with their sandwich boxes just to the left of the beer tent. "They're all in the top year and they're leaving us on Friday," Philip Mallon, deputy head of Old Hall Juniors confided. "Normally we'd just take them ten-pin bowling as an end-of-year treat. But the World Cup Final has suddenly given them an enthusiasm for cricket."

A girl called Evie stood up at that point and told me that she was going to be at the T-20 match with her family on the Saturday and she was really looking forward to it. Hope she did enjoy it because, as it transpired, Derbyshire would win that one by five wickets. Here, however, they had just lost by 72 runs, Rampaul having heaved one to Bavuma at square leg off the bowling of Ben Sanderson.

As the players trudged off for a slightly early lunch and some premature bag-packing, the outfield filled with youngsters playing impromptu matches and old-timers making seemingly judicious studies of the strip on which an improbable number of wickets had fallen on what might have been termed "Mad Monday".

Back in the Brampton tent, meanwhile, there was a pronounced movement not just to the bar but to the second-hand book stall to its right. Everything was a quid, including Duncan Hamilton's memorable biography of Harold Larwood and an unsullied hardback called *More Than A Game, the story of cricket*, by one John Major.

There seemed to be a disproportionate number of Dickies in stock – books by and about Dickie Bird, that is. The celebrated umpire was among many former cricketing luminaries quoted in the centre spread of the festival's 2019 souvenir brochure. He recalled being out in the middle with Sachin Tendulkar "stood at the side of me".

"Do you know, Dickie," Sachin had remarked, "I don't think I've ever seen a more beautiful cricketing setting than this." That must have been some time after Tendulkar's first visit in 1990 when he'd scored 108 not out for India against Derbyshire. He was 16 at the time.

Dickie's old friend and verbal sparring partner Geoffrey Boycott recalled playing here on many memorable occasions, but particularly on July 6, 1970. "It was a lovely sunny day and a super atmosphere. I was on 99 not out and at the end of the over Mike Page said to me, 'Chris Wilkins is coming on to bowl and he gets wickets from nowhere. Be careful, Fiery.' I cut his first ball perfectly for a certain boundary only for Edwin Smith to dive full length and catch it inches from the ground . . . Forty years on I appreciate the beauty of Queen's Park much more than I did on that day."

The brochure carried eulogies to the Chesterfield festival from many another cricketing legend, including those heroes of Headingley '81 Ian Botham and Bob Willis. The latter had "fond memories of battles with several Derbyshire players, including Geoff (Dusty) Miller, who is one of cricket's real gentlemen".

And a local lad, what's more. "Dusty" was born in Chesterfield in 1952, went to the town's grammar school and, for a while, ran the Moss and Miller sporting goods emporium with local football legend Ernie Moss. Oh yes, and he also took 60 wickets in 34 Test Matches for England, became an OBE, England selector and President of Derbyshire, the county for which he took 888 wickets in 283 first-class matches between 1973 and 1990.

He will always be remembered, however, for Melbourne Test on Boxing Day, 1982. Australia needed only three runs to win with their last wicket standing when Jeff Thomson edged a ball from Botham into the slip cordon. Chris Tavarre spilled it but Miller managed to hold on to the rebound before it hit the ground. Cue pandemonium.

Simon Hughes, former Middlesex bowler and now author and editor of The Cricketer, described Miller in 1990 as "the only remaining player who unfailingly visited the opposing team's dressing room after play to thank them for the game . . . and the last man to field at slip with a whoopee cushion up his jumper".

Not, presumably, on the occasion when he took that catch Down Under in 1982 – although there may have been plenty of whooping around him.

Useful spinner that he was, Miller was not in the same class as Shane Warne. Few were. The Australian who introduced himself to the Test scene by turning a ball "twice the width of Mike Gatting" had evidently visited Chesterfield on at least one occasion. Dressing room attendant Edwin Clarke remembered it all too well. "He got me to nip to the bookies for him," he recalled when we met up in the pavilion. Edwin was filling a black plastic bag with detritus while one or two of the players lingered over lunch and I was being shown around by John Windle, secretary of the Friends.

Particularly memorable was the panoramic view from the front window where the scorers had been sitting at their computers. Spread out before them, at an angle un-paralleled by any other seat in the ground, was a pitch harbouring so many memories of great players past.

Needless to say, W.G. Grace had turned up. On that occasion he was playing for a London County side against Derbyshire. In 1904, as it happened, the same year that Essex also came to town and one Percy Perrin had made 343 not out for them, 272 of those runs coming in boundaries. Don Bradman had graced the place in 1930 and '34, the days when touring sides started at Worcester and went around the counties as well as the Test grounds. Ramadhin and Valentine may have been immortalised in a calypso song, but it was Derbyshire's Cliff Gladwin who stole the headlines here in 1950 by taking six for 40 in the West Indies first innings.

The crooked spire would have looked down on it all. And there it was, revealed at last, to the right of the trees that had obscured its presence from most of the ground.

We had a much closer view of that most extraordinary local landmark an hour or so later. Once Allister had stocked up on Derbyshire oat cakes from a splendid cheese shop in the market place, we finished up in The Rectory.

No, we weren't having tea with the rector. We were having a pint in a pub of that name. It was close to the bus station as well as the churchyard, though the wall around the pub garden ensured that we had a better view of the spire than the 65A to Buxton.

We were, needless to say, en route to the railway station. But unlike our arrival, the departure could wait a bit longer. There was no great hurry. "Another pint?"

"Oh, go on then."

* Northamptonshire beat Derbyshire by 72 runs half way through day three.

The park in full festive glory – a setting that sent Sachin Tendulkar into eulogies

The spire peering over the trees and still visible from the scorers' box

Pictures: John Windle

69

Pick up a folding chair and sit where you like . . .

Chapter Six

College Ground, Cheltenham

Gloucestershire v Worcestershire, day two, Monday July 22

The couple in front of me seemed a bit different from the majority of those queuing patiently at the side of the school chapel. For a start they were young and looked "cool", as young people say. For another thing, they were talking to each other in a language that seemed double Dutch to me.

It turned out to be what you might call "single Dutch". Kai Meissen, 25, and Anne Cillekens, 23, were from Holland. "We've been in Wales for a week and we just wanted to see some English things before we head home," said Kai, switching effortlessly to English, as the Dutch tend to do.

"No, we don't know anything about cricket," he added in answer to my obvious question. "But I guess we'll learn the rules by looking them up on our phones."

"Might take you most of the day," I warned them. But, no, I didn't add that it might seem double Dutch to them. Instead I confirmed that the scene inside would be as English as they come. Once we'd finally made it to the single tented turnstile at the side of the gate admitting members. "Queuing patiently is another very English thing," I assured them.

At least the number of people trying to get in just after 11 on a Monday morning was a sign of the ongoing popularity of the longest surviving cricket festival of all.

Gloucestershire had first pitched up at Cheltenham in 1872 at the behest of the founder, one James Lillywhite, who had become what you might call a cricket entrepreneur and administrator as well as being coach at the college. The county side beat Surrey by an innings and 37 runs largely thanks to a haul of 12 wickets for 63 by one W.G. Grace. The "Doctor", as he then wasn't, hit the first triple century in a county match three years later by scoring 318 not out here against Yorkshire.

Other legends of "Glorse", as the county's called in its more rustic retreats, left their mark on Cheltenham – literally so in the case of Gilbert Jessop who apparently smashed a window in the nearby hospital while wielding his bat with characteristic gusto. Jessop was born in Cheltenham and went to the local grammar school. Not that he seemed to hang around too long on his return to town with the county. He took just 18 minutes to reach 51 on the College Ground in 1895 against Yorkshire. An even faster 50 came in 15 minutes against Hampshire in 1907.

Fast forward to 1928 and Walter Hammond, better known as "Wally", scored 139 in the first innings and 143 in the second. And in a brief break from batting, he took ten catches in the same match against Surrey.

Over 90 years on and Gloucestershire had already beaten Leicestershire by six wickets in the first County Championship game of the 2019 festival. Cheltenham is blessed with two, interspersed with a couple of Vitality Blasts, and followed by three under-19 one-day internationals. Today was the second of four days against visitors from just over the border.

Worcestershire shared with Gloucestershire the privilege of having once had on their books yet another cricketing legend whose classic batting style was much talked about in my early lifetime. My Dad, a man of Warwickshire, used to almost purr with pleasure when Tom Graveney appeared on our grainy black-and-white telly playing a cover drive for England.

Like all great batsmen, his reputation has stood the test of time. I hadn't been in the ground five minutes when I heard his name being mentioned with due reverence.

By that time I'd already checked that everything was in its place — the scoreboard on which Gloucestershire were 349 for nine (tick); outline of the Cotswolds rising majestically above the advertising hoardings (tick); the golden stones of the college chapel flexing their buttressed frontage like a symbol of muscular Christianity (tick); the twin towers of the school gymnasium harbouring the pavilion that Jack Russell had once told me was rather dark inside, "like a dungeon with showers"(tick); tent selling Jack's paintings . . . er, no. For some reason the former England wicket keeper wasn't here on this, the most evocative "home" ground of his former county.

Still, Tony Sanders had come with the book stall that I'd last browsed around in Tunbridge Wells. And there were plenty of food vans and stalls to choose from come lunchtime.

One van, offering the appealing prospect of "Woozy Pig" with "dirty fries", was parked near the two genial gents who had been discussing Tom Graveney. Among other things. The conversation ranged from the era of "tubbier cricketers" such as the two Colins, Cowdrey and Milburn, to Tom Smith's slow advance to 82 out in the middle. "He's added one in the last half hour," one of them observed before going on to discuss the huge crowd here for the visit of Middlesex (Compton, Edrich and all) to Cheltenham in the glorious summer of 1947.

That was two years before I was born and neither of the genial gents looked old enough to have been here in person. Nor would they have been here, I suspect, to see Graveney bat against the West Indies in 1950.

Even the late Frank Keating was only 12, as he recalled in one of his memorable pieces of lyrical journalism spun for the sports pages of The Guardian. This one was written in 2003 when Graveney was still alive and living in Cheltenham. Hope he read it.

He would have been 22 on the hot August day in 1950 when he ambled out to bat against "the magical guiles of Sonny Ramadhin and Alf Valentine". As Frank went on to recall, Graveney was the only one to play them with any degree of certainty — "coltishly upright and gangly shy at the crease, but with a high, twirly back-lift and a stirring signature flourish in the follow-through of his trademark cover-drive. A man sitting sardined on the grass nest to me in the rapt throng said: 'Our Tom'll be servin' England within a twelvemonth, you'll see'."

"And so he was, and so we did."

Time, perhaps, to return to the Cheltenham Festival of 2019. There were a couple of fabled names on the scorecard: Hammond for Gloucestershire and d'Oliveira for Worcestershire. Brett d'Olivieira happened to be grandson of the great Basil. He would make a gutsy contribution to Worcestershire's revival later in the day.

Miles Hammond had last popped up at Arundel and, as I pointed out in that chapter, he is not a descendant of Walter. He was born in Cheltenham, however, and only the previous year he'd been the first Hammond to score a century there (103 against Sussex) since Wally's 178 in 1937. Against Worcestershire, as it happened, the county that was about to respond to "Glorse's" 354 all out. Smith had added one more run before being caught by Ed Barnard off Joe Leach for 83.

That was only one fewer than his contribution to Gloucestershire's impressive total of 500-plus for nine against Leicestershire in the previous four-day festival match. "Seems like he's been in all week," somebody sighed as I set off in search of Light. John Light, that is, who had been chairman of Gloucestershire when I'd first come to Cheltenham on a gloriously sunny day in 2013.

Kent had been the visitors on that occasion and, on a prolific wicket for batting, both sides had made hay. There had been boundaries galore and adventurous declarations as well as entertaining conversations in the officials' enclosure into which I had somehow blagged my way. I remember John telling me how, in pre-war days, Saturdays watching cricket at Cheltenham had been the only annual holidays taken by Cotswold foresters such as his father – a cousin of Laurie Lee's, no less, another great Gloucestershire spinner. Of words rather than balls, I might add about the lad from Slad who wrote such mesmerising prose about his days in pre-war England and war-torn Spain.

Six years on I was stealthily edging my way past the front of the pavilion when John, suitably suited and booted, came strolling past in the other direction. "I'm vice-president of the club these days," he confided. "A benign elder statesman," he added as Worcestershire's Callum Ferguson was caught in the slips. By Hammond off David Payne, the public address system proclaimed.

"Now there's a name to conjure with," the vice-president murmured dreamily. Somehow I suspect he meant Hammond rather than Ferguson or Payne. Then he went on to tell me that the crowd the previous day had been around 3,000. "And I reckon there are nearly as many today."

Certainly there didn't appear to be too many empty seats, I noticed, as John sauntered on and the poplar trees began to sway in the summer breeze. Which reminded me. Somewhere on this ground is a tree dedicated to one Percy Jeeves, the Warwickshire bowler who was killed on the Somme in 1916. A century on it was planted in his memory by the P.G. Wodehouse Society. Wodehouse had seen Jeeves at the Cheltenham Festival of 2013, just at the end of cricket's "Golden Age" that preceded the horrors of World War One.

The author liked the cut of Jeeves's jib. Or at least his bowling action. Remembered his name, too, when he was living in New York and evidently delving into his memories of Cheltenham. Jeeves may have died in unspeakable horror but his name would be immortalised as the unflappable valet of the scrape-prone Bertie Wooster.

P.G. Wodehouse. Laurie Lee. Whoever next?

Bill Greenoff was not a literary figure, as far as I know. He seemed to know a fair bit about cricket grounds, mind you. "I've seen first-class cricket on 55 of them," he told me when we fell into conversation by chance as he stood outside the pavilion waiting for a phone call.

That seemed an unlikely figure until I remembered that there were over 60 outgrounds alone in the early 1960s. Over 50 years on there were far fewer, but Bill had evidently managed to visit a fair number in the meantime. He'd worked as a rep for his wife's needle-craft company. "If you were canny, you could get the job done in the morning and get to a cricket ground by early afternoon," he smiled wistfully.

In his later years he worked part-time as a "hospital driver". Indeed he had just dropped off a patient for treatment at the building, handily placed across the road, where not only Jessop but Hammond and Graham Gooch had all landed balls through the windows or into the grounds during festivals past. "As soon as she rings, I've got to be off," he said.

At least there seemed to be no threat to the hospital from flying sixes this morning. Worcestershire's top order appeared to be a little tied down by the Gloucestershire "quicks". The only time I raised my eyes skyward was to observe an intrusive tower block that had the effrontery to . . . well, tower over the far end of the college chapel. Built in 1968, apparently, for the Eagle Star insurance company.

"At least it's not black glass and there's a recognisable toning of the colours," said Bill, who evidently had a feeling for the aesthetics of cricket. He'd just been waxing lyrical about his visit to the Isle of Wight where Hampshire had played for the first time since 1962 when the phone rang. His patient was ready for collection.

I'd hear more about Newclose during the lunch interval. For now I was steadily wending my way around a ground bordered by many a tent. In one I spotted Gloucestershire's eminent cricket historian Roger Gibbons holding forth. Just the man I'd been looking for.

It was Roger who had told me stories about Jessop and Hammond, Grace and Graveney when I'd first come here in 2013. And it was Roger who'd witnessed Gooch's huge heave into the hospital grounds.

"I'd been sitting close to the boundary at the far end with my Dad and the game was going nowhere," he recalled when we met up again. Gooch had been fielding for Essex at long-off and, as is the way with festivals, he'd seemed happy to chat with members of the crowd. "'We'll be in soon and we'll have a bit of fun'," said Gibbons quoting Gooch. "Sure enough, he picked up the first bad ball and off it went. Wow . . "

For a moment Roger's words trailed away in a fog of fond reminiscence. He'd first come to the Cheltenham Festival, aged six, on a bus from Stroud. And, yes, he was with his Dad. It was 1950 and, yes, it was the same match against the West Indies that the 12-year-old Frank Keating had witnessed. Yes, he remembered Graveney batting against Ramadhin and Valentine.

But, typically, he also remembered something more obscure: "[John] Mortimore came in for [Tom] Goddard on the morning of the match and two scorecards were printed." Also typically, the historian still has those scorecards and, generously, he later sent them to be reprinted here (see pages 85-86).

Mortimore would have been just 17 when that evidently memorable match took place before a packed house at Cheltenham. Goddard would have been 49. Yet only three seasons previously the huge-handed spinner had taken 206 County Championship wickets, which remains a record in that competition to this day. His partnership with Charlie Parker had been one of the most lethal combinations in the county game.

Charlie Parker? Now there was a name to conjure with. It was one of many that started spilling from the lips of venerable members sharing the tent with Roger. What about George Emmett and Jack Crapp? And don't forget the incomparable Bryan Wells, better known as "Bomber". Liked his lunch and tea-time tucker did Bomber. Indeed he would have qualified for the "tubby cricketers" club that we'd been discussing on the other side of the ground.

Here in the tent somebody remembered a story about his first game for the county in 1951. "He was sitting in a park in Gloucester with his lady friend when a bloke got out of a car, strolled over and said: 'Are you Wells?' Bomber nodded. 'You're playing tomorrow.' So he got on the bus the following day. When he finally came on to bowl, he was kept on for more than 20 overs and took five or six wickets . . "

"Five," Roger put in quietly.

"....Bomber used to come in off about the two paces. When he was finally taken off, he told the captain, 'If I'm going to be kept on that long again, I'm going to have to cut down my run-up.'"

Cue laughter and cue the entrance of a man sporting a Cheltenham Festival t-shirt, a peaked cap and a bag. "I've got a Jessop for you," he whispered to the historian before groping in the said bag and coming out with everything from a Day and Mason cricket magazine from 1949 (1s/6d) to a pamphlet for Courtney Walsh's benefit match in 1992. "John's a bit of a scavenger," Roger explained before "the Jessop" finally emerged. It turned out to be a scorecard from Gilbert's early playing days in club cricket.

I left them poring over the various ancient treasures on a white-clothed table with an open bottle of red perched precariously in the middle.

Lunchtime was approaching and Worcestershire were 40 for two, having added 15 since the fall of the last wicket. Tempted as I was by the cold buffet on offer for 12 quid at the Cow Corner Inn beer tent, I needed to be in another nearby tent to hear one of the free interval talks that are part of the offer at Cheltenham.

Last year we'd been greatly entertained by former Lancashire chief executive Jim Cumbes, the last man to play in a one-day final at Lord's (for Worcestershire) and a League Cup Final at Wembley (for Aston Villa). Jim had been invited back again and would be talking at tea-time. For now, though, Paul Edwards was holding forth on a subject dear to my heart.

The cricket correspondent of *The Times* was presenting a eulogy to cricket festivals. He'd managed to spend not one but four days at watching Lancashire and at Sedbergh School (see Chapter Four) and had written an evocative spread about it in *The Cricketer*, as I discovered when the August edition came thrusting through our letter box.

In his talk he also waxed lyrical about the Newclose Ground in the Isle of Wight that had so impressed Bill Greenoff whom I'd met outside the pavilion here all of half an hour ago. According to Paul, it had "a pavilion modelled on Wormsley, a scoreboard modelled on The Oval and pavilion seating modelled on Lord's". And now it was up for sale, as the entrepreneur-philanthropist behind it, Brian Gardener, had died six years after it opened. All of which gave me another pang of regret that it hadn't made it there in May to see Hampshire play.

As is the way with lunchtime talks, they can rarely be confined entirely to the lunch interval. Questions for the speaker went on. So did the applause. Then there was another round of applause. And another. Both came from the crowd beyond the tent. Worcestershire, it seemed, had lost two quick wickets. "Oh God," said Paul, "I'm supposed to be covering this."

As he rushed back to the press box, Gloucestershire supporters clustered around the scoreboard were already discussing the prospect of enforcing a follow-on. For me there was something else to discuss. I'd managed to grab a quick word with Chris Coley who not only chairs the interval talks but co-ordinates the entire festival.

"I've been doing it for over 30 years," he said blithely, implying that it was not much more than a hobby that he loved, before going on to remind me that "this was a school field two weeks ago and it wouldn't be used all summer were it not for the festival. We're lucky insofar as the school has a proper cricket groundsman in Christian Brain. He's from the brewery family apparently." (That would be Brain's of Cardiff, as I recall from many a heady day and night in the Welsh capital.) "Christian came here from Rad. . ."

"Radlett? Where Middlesex played earlier this summer?"

"No, Radley College in Oxfordshire."

Here at Cheltenham College in Gloucestershire Chris had evidently established the necessary financial backing through his corporate hospitality company, as I discovered on Googling his name. He also had strong links with the other festival for which this affluent and elegant spa is known on both sides of the Irish Sea. Which explains why the main sponsor of this year's cricket festival was one Fergal O'Brien, better known for training fast horses in the Cotswolds than fast bowlers in the nets.

There was a whole stall bedecked with photographs of his many winners, I noticed, as I strolled back to the Cow Corner Inn, conscious that it had been a very long time since breakfast and hopeful that the cold buffet was still available.

It was. Just about. The girl behind the counter managed to scrape together some pasta salad, mackerel pate, a slice or two of ham and a couple of rolls. All of which I saw off with a pint of St Austell Tribute at a table just beyond the confines of the tent awning. It was spread with another immaculately white table cloth and offered a view of the afternoon's play. Just after 2.45, with plateful and pint long since seen off, Worcestershire were 66 for five. Ben Cox had just been caught by Benny Howell bowled David Payne for an unlucky 13. The enforced follow-on was looking more and more likely.

"This is the worst Worcestershire batting line-up I've seen in 60 years," said a man with a slight Black Country accent, sporting a shirt with a West Bromwich Albion badge. He was there with a mate and their wives, one of whom leaned over to me as Albion man went to the bar and advised, "Don't mention the Wolves to him. That'll really get him started."

Wouldn't dream of it, Madam. I was more interested in hearing about his reminiscences of Tom Graveney at New Road, Worcester, and, indeed, Basil d'Oliviera – bearing in mind that his grandson had just joined Ross Whiteley at the wicket.

As the afternoon went on, the sun came out and Worcestershire dug in. Not entirely tediously, it should be said. As the sun's rays grew stronger so did some of the strokes. Whiteley suddenly struck a six over midwicket at around 10 past three. Not quite of Jessop, Gooch or Hammond proportions, but a welcome boost all the same for Worcestershire's long-suffering supporters.

He'd reached his 50 just before tea and the next time I checked the scoreboard, Worcestershire had advanced to 188 without further loss and d'Oliviera was on 54.

By then I'd re-joined the Black Country quartet after another tea-time session of entertaining Cumbes reminiscences followed by a short sermon on the spiritual nature of cricket from a clergyman that I'd starting talking to by chance outside what you might call the talks tent.

Albion man was soon in full flow when I reminded him about the days when Worcestershire used to play at Dudley. Today we think of the unofficial capital of the Black Country as being just another part of the West Midlands. But under the pre-1974 system it was part of an island of Worcestershire surrounded by a sea of Staffordshire.

The county side had made their last visit for a John Player League match in 1977, by which time alarming cracks had been found in a ground that had been laid out above former limestone workings. It closed for good a few years later.

Admittedly the remains of a mediaeval castle had been clearly visible from that former out-ground. But it was also surrounded by factories and foundries. So why were we reminiscing about Dudley while sitting here in the sedate setting of the Cheltenham College ground?

That's cricket. That's England.

Heaven only knows what the Dutch couple that I'd met on the way into the ground would have made of it.

* Gloucestershire beat Worcestershire by 13 runs two days later.

The golden stones of the college chapel

The twin towers of the school gymnasium that doubles as the pavilion

Tony Hickey

Impromptu matches are allowed on the hallowed turf of the College Ground during the lunch and tea intervals

On the front foot with hanging basket in full bloom behind

Pictures by Tony Hickey

Two scorecards from Gloucestershire's 1950 match against the West Indies with John Mortimore on one and Tom Goddard on the other

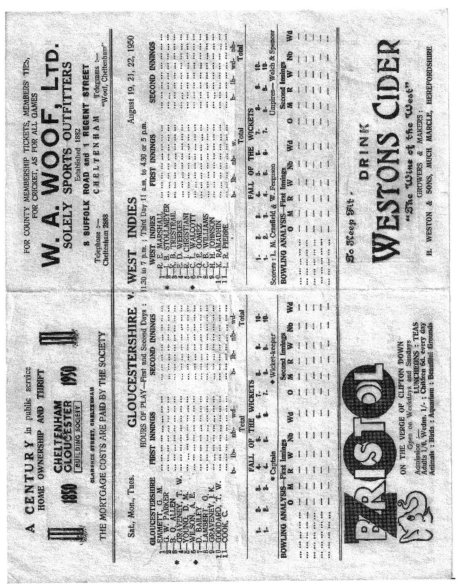

Scorecards donated by Roger Gibbons

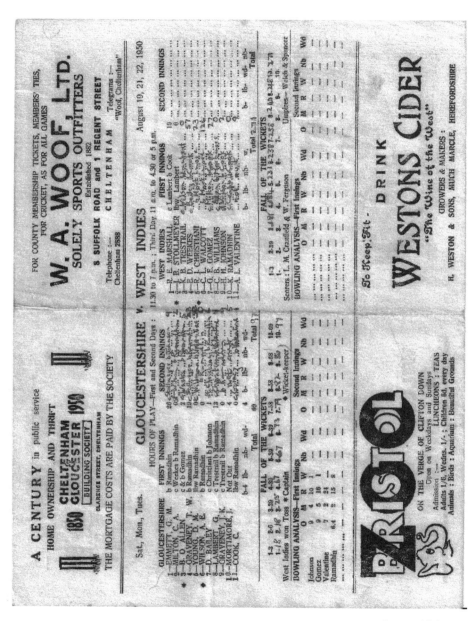

Roger Gibbons

Chapter Seven

North Marine Road, Scarborough

Yorkshire v Nottinghamshire, day three, Tuesday August 20

Dickie Bird looked tanned enough to suggest that he'd just returned from a holiday in Barbados rather than spent a few days watching cricket in Scarborough. A very brown Bird indeed. But then come to think of it, he had spent much of his life in the open air, first as a cricketer with Yorkshire and Leicestershire, later as a fabled umpire and more recently as a spectator.

Now 87, he still seemed a very chirpy Bird. Well, he was sitting outside the lengthy hospitality marquee after a no-doubt decent lunch. And Yorkshire were in a seemingly unassailable position on the field. Having dismissed Nottinghamshire for 184, they were 350 runs ahead by mid-afternoon with three wickets still in hand.

"They're batting too long," Dickie declared. "You never know about the weather in England."

Not that he would be here for the final day. Whatever the weather, he had to go back home to Barnsley and then head for Headingley where the third Ashes Test was due to start on Thursday. Neither of us knew at the time that the fourth day would perhaps surpass Headingley '81 as the greatest England comeback of all-time. For now we were both happy here at North Marine Road, a setting that combines intimacy and homeliness with a sense of being in a small-scale stadium. "First-class cricket on holiday," as the Yorkshire cricket writer J.M. (Jim) Kilburn once put it.

"Is it your favourite festival ground?" I asked the venerable Bird.

"Oh, yes, without a shadow of doubt. It's the best outground in the world – the pitch, the outfield, the atmosphere. As a batsman, you graft for the first hour. After that you dip your bread. I saw (Don) Bradman here in 1948 when the place was packed to the rafters. And I still enjoy coming, to this day. When I was umpiring, I used to look at the fixtures at the start of the season and when I saw that I was down for Yorkshire at Scarborough that was marvellous."

Playing for Yorkshire at Scarborough had not always been quite so pleasurable. Particularly 60 years ago, after they'd just won the Championship against Sussex at Hove. The following day they had to be here on the North Yorkshire coast to play the MCC. "No motorways in those days," Dickie recalled. He'd covered the 312 miles in a car shared with spinner Don Wilson.

"We got here about four in the morning and went for a celebratory drink at the (long-demolished) Balmoral Hotel. A few hours later the whole team set off from there towards North Marine Road. Thousands of people were lining the streets and the ground was chock-a-block when we finally got here. Then we had to pose for photos out in the middle. In those days matches started at 11.30. I remember looking at the clock and noticing that it was 20 to 12."

Dickie was 12th man for much of that time when Yorkshire's formidable side included the likes of Brian Close, Fred Trueman and Ray Illingworth. Finally making it into the first team and playing at his most beloved outground had its painful moments – not least when he found himself facing the formidable Frank "Typhoon" Tyson.

"He was quicker than this feller (Jofra) Archer, you know. Quicker than Dennis Lillee or Jeff Thomson, for that matter; or Malcolm Marshall or Michael Holding. But I managed to hit him for three fours in a row. Through the covers, just here," he added pointing to the boundary a few yards from where we were sitting.

Tyson was not happy. "'Try hitting this so-and-so for four,' he told me before hurtling in from the Trafalgar Road end. I'd got all my weight on the front foot, full of confidence, until that vicious bouncer reared up and hit me on the side of the head. Of course, there were no helmets then."

Dickie was duly despatched to hospital. "They stitched me up and, later on, I came back to finish my innings."

Did you suffer from concussion?

"Don't think they knew what it was in those days."

Health and safety, eh?

I left the brown Bird in good cheer before heading back in search of two old mates and long-time Notts supporters. One was Allister Craddock, whom I'd last met up with at the Chesterfield festival all of a month ago. The other was the cartoonist Pete Dredge whose witty works have appeared in *Private Eye* and *Punch*, the *New Statesman* and the *Spectator*. Among others. Pete recently moved to Scarborough with his wife Sharon, having once had a holiday apartment on North Marine Road itself, with the sea to the rear and Trafalgar Square just around the corner.

No Nelson's column there, needless to say. Just plenty of hotels and boarding houses that looked somewhat grander at the front than from the rear. One of the more homely aspects of this small-scale stadium is catching a glimpse of someone hanging out a line of washing in a back yard just to the right and slightly above the electronic scoreboard.

The rear windows of those boarding houses have been under threat from flying balls since Yorkshire played their first championship match here in 1896 – and probably for some time before that. The festival's founder, C.I. 'Buns' Thornton, had been a renowned clouter. It's said that he once lofted a straight drive over one of those houses and into Trafalgar Square itself.

Cec Pepper did something similar while hitting 168 in 146 minutes for the Australian Services XI here in 1945. And Dickie had recalled another Aussie, Richie Benaud no less, cracking a six into a boarding-house back wall.

But there'd been "surprisingly little damage" to adjoining windows in recent seasons, I'd been assured by Scarborough CC chairman Paul Harrand when we'd met in the hospitality tent shortly before the start of play.

He'd kindly taken time off from trying to get the public address system to work to sit down and reminisce about his home ground. Paul had played here for many years, starting in the mid-'90s, but he could go back a lot further than that. "When I was a young boy, I remember being handed a bucket on a blistering hot day and being asked to go up and down the wooden bench seats on the popular bank to ask for donations to John Hampshire's benefit year. By the time we'd finished, there were four buckets and they were all full."

The young Harrand had also been called upon to ferry beer and lager to the press box – a somewhat taxing task in those more bibulous days of journalism. (Even more so had it been in John Arlott's time when there would have had to be a bottle of claret or three as well as the cans.)

Covering Yorkshire at Scarborough then and now must have been a lot more fun for cricket writers than covering Yorkshire at Headingley. Like all great Test arenas, the latter lacks atmosphere for county matches. "It's very echoey, looks empty and the West Stand is usually closed," Paul recalled. "But North Marine Road is the best attended outground in the country by a long way. The boundaries are close in and the crowd feels part of the action.

"It can be quite intimidating for the players, mind you. I remember talking to former Warwickshire captain Neil Smith recently and he recalled how he used to tell 'the lads' that Scarborough was 'like a Colosseum' where you're 'thrown to the lions'."

Pretty good pitch to bat on, mind you. (Always has been since the likes of Hobbs and Hutton scored double centuries here for the Players against the Gents.) And over the past decade, Scarborough's John Dodds has been voted the English Cricket Board's best outgrounds Groundsman of the Year on numerous occasions.

"We've had an agreement with Yorkshire since 2010 for 10 days of cricket here," Paul went on. "But over the past four or five years we've had to make do with eight days. Thanks to changes in the fixtures schedule, one day games are played at different times from Country Championship matches."

Yet his own most vivid memory of a match on his own club ground was Darren Lehmann belting Yorkshire's highest one-day score of all time in 2001. The Australian's 191 included 11 sixes and 24 fours. "I felt," Paul mused, "as though I was watching something truly extraordinary."

Against Nottinghamshire, as it happened. Which reminded me. Wasn't I looking for the old friends with whom I'd spent many a Test match at Trent Bridge?

By the time I finally located Messrs Craddock and Dredge again, fat seagulls were gathering on the Scarborough outfield like vultures hovering over the corpse of Notts. It was 3.20pm and, by a strange coincidence, Yorkshire were exactly 320 for nine. Batting at number eight, the South African Keshav Maharaj evidently felt that it was time to open his shoulders. One of three sixes in his entertaining 35 landed to our right, scattering the gulls and smacking against a wall behind the beer bar.

The famous Scarborough tea bar was located just behind us. Conveniently so. We nipped in just before the rush when Maharaj was caught and bowled and the home side were all out for 338.

The tea bar's walls were still covered with sketches of Boycott and Binks, Hirst and Hutton, as well as many another Yorkshire cricketing legend. And the portions were still substantial. I set about an enormous slice of chocolate cake with a plastic spoon rather than a pastry fork. After all, this was Scarborough not Cheltenham or the Ladies' Pavilion at Worcester.

On the far side of a field packed with tea-time wicket inspectors and impromptu children's matches, a sea breeze was setting flags a-flutter to the left of the red-bricked and steep-roofed late-Victorian pavilion. It was to that very building that Ricky Ponting returned after scoring a seemingly effortless century for Somerset on his championship debut in July, 2004. He was not happy after losing his concentration for a moment and giving his wicket away to spinner Richard Dawson. As Duncan Hamilton recalled in his wonderful book *A Last English Summer*, the great Australian batsman "took the pavilion steps two at a time, threw his bat against the wall and simultaneously uttered a long, loud oath which could be heard throughout the pavilion. The oath rhymed with clucking bell. There are few secrets on such an intimate ground."

Allister, Pete and myself might even have heard it had we been sitting where we had been at start of play this morning – not far from the pavilion and just beyond the sight screen, albeit 15 years after Ricky's rant. What we could hear was much munching amid the chunter. Despite a lengthy walk to the ground, I wasn't remotely hungry, having seen off a full English breakfast at the hotel where I'd been staying with my wife Jackie.

Those around us were evidently not so fortunate. "I always want to eat when I go to the cricket," someone behind was confiding to his mates while opening a packet of crisps shortly after 11 am. "Oh God, they're super-hot chilli-flavoured."

Not only super-hot but super-sized, as a glance behind revealed. Despite the heat, he manfully crunched through crisps plucked from an enormous bag before embarking on the first of many sandwiches.

Meanwhile, a chap with a stick and a floppy hat strolled past biting the end of the chocolate flake protruding from a huge vanilla cornet and the man sitting on the row in front of us set about a large iced bun topped with a cherry and stuffed with cream. He too was sporting a hat. A straw one, as it happened, ringed with a band advertising Bradford and Bingley on one side and Canterbury on the other. Canterbury Building Society rather than Canterbury cricket ground, one assumed, judging by his accent.

"Tha's playing the wrong game," he bawled at Nottinghamshire's Luke Fletcher at one point, in a brief break from biting his bun. Fletcher had rather cleverly flicked up the ball with his boot and seemed at one point to be engaged in demonstrating his footballing abilities through playing "keepy-uppy". Mind you, he finished the Yorkshire innings with figures of five for 67, despite having confided to Allister while fielding on the boundary that "there are a lot of dead bowlers under that wicket".

Certainly batsmen have prospered here. You have to go back 120 years to come across a bowler taking almost certainly the best figures on this ground – nine for 24 for CI Thornton's XI against the Australians. That was one Wilfred Rhodes, the great left-arm spinner who replaced Bobby Peel when the latter was finally dismissed by Lord Hawke "for presenting himself on the pitch in a state of intoxication".

A whole wall was dedicated to Hawke, the "father of Yorkshire cricket", in an entertaining stall-cum-museum that I discovered on my first stroll of the day around the Scarborough ground. His predecessor as captain had been a player rather than a gent. "Talented but unruly, this was the Yorkshire of 1875," it says on another wall. "Not surprisingly, no-one wanted the responsibility of being captain. In the absence of a gentleman, Tom Emmett drew the short straw."

Nearby is a quote from the most celebrated of cricket writers, Sir Neville Cardus of the "Manchester" Guardian, as that esteemed organ of liberal values was known in his day. Despite Old Trafford being his home ground, Cardus was not ungenerous to the county across the Pennines. "The Yorkshireman's intolerance of an enemy's prowess," he wrote, "is simply the measure of the Yorkshireman's pride in his county's genius for cricket."

Lunchtime was approaching when I stepped out of the mini-museum to take in the view from the pathway behind the steep rows of weathered wooden benches packed with proud Yorkshiremen. Distant hills rose above rooftops of slate. Gulls circled and swooped in the fresh sea air.

Despite or perhaps because of my recent proximity to crisp-munchers and bun-stuffers, I still didn't fancy much for lunch. That may explain why the chocolate cake in the tea bar still looms so large in my recollections of this memorable day. For now I could not be seduced by the offer of a "wood-fired" pizza, a Bratwurst frankfurter, roast pork with "fresh-cooked" chips, nor even a pork pie with mushy peas and mint sauce. "Goose Fair peas", in other words. That's what they used to be called during my days in Nottingham when peas and mint sauce represented the *pièce de résistance* in many a pub.

Pub?

Now that's what I did fancy: a pint.

Yorkshire had just lost their fifth wicket for 232 when Harry Brook had been caught by Jake Ball off Liam Patterson-White for 18. It was time to pick up a pass-out ticket and follow Pete, now a resident of Scarborough rather than Nottingham. A few hundred yards up North Marine Road we strode before turning sharp right through the doorway of The Albert.

A wise choice as it turned out. This pub served the finest pint of Tetley's that I've savoured for many a year. "Born" [rather than brewed] in Leeds," said a sign near the bar. The brewery itself was closed down by Carlsberg in 2011, five years after the dray horses that had once been part of the city's fabric had been put out to grass.

But never mind Leeds. We were enjoying a festive day at the seaside. So we took our pints out to the front terrace where we fell into conversation with one Peter Smith, a retired finance director, who was soon reminiscing about his childhood in Huddersfield and his tram trip to the 1948 Test match at Headingley.

Back to Leeds again then.

"I got up at the crack of dawn and was at the ground by 10 to eight," Peter recalled. "But the queues outside were so long even at that time that I couldn't get a seat. Finished up sitting on a pile of bricks."

No, he didn't see Bradman bat. But he remembered to this day "the stillness and quiet" that prevailed among the massed ranks of that post-war crowd as Len Hutton and Cyril Washbrook built a first-innings stand of 168.

At this point his story was interrupted by a seagull depositing crap on the shoulders of Allister, as if to comment on Nottinghamshire's chances of saving the game here at Scarborough.

As the afternoon wore on and the chocolate cake went down, victory for Yorkshire began to look inevitable. No respite from the weather, which was set fair for tomorrow as well.

By 5 o'clock Notts were 51 for three when Joe Clarke was caught by Jonny Tattersall off Maharaj for four. Admittedly there was some late resistance from Ben Duckett, who was not out 47 at the close and Chris Nash whose 30 included a memorable cover drive that may well have had Dickie Bird chirping as it jumped over the boundary rope in front of the hospitality tent.

On the walk back to the hotel, I paused to peer at some cricketing pictures in the window of a gallery not far beyond The Albert. In the window was a picture of Dickie in his umpiring prime. At Scarborough what's more. .

What a privilege it had been to discuss memories of Scarborough with him this afternoon. And what a day it had been. On my walk to the ground this morning I'd come across a bloke sporting an England straw hat and a New Zealand t-shirt.

"They were selling these [t-shirts] at three for 10 quid when I came to the festival here last year," said Mike ("the Bike") Rose, an inveterate motorcyclist now in his 70s. "And New Zealand were always my second team, even before the World Cup final."

Mike had spoken in an accent that owed nothing to Notts or Yorkshire. Turned out that he came from Kidderminster and supported Worcestershire. "We played here during last year's festival and watching cricket at Scarborough had always been on my bucket list," he went on. "I'd never been to a cricket ground with an atmosphere like it. So I told my wife 'I'm going back again next year, even if Worcester aren't playing'."

I never saw Mike the Bike at close of play. But somehow I suspect that he thought the journey was well worth the effort.

For me it was the end of a much longer journey that had begun at Guildford in early June. On the way I'd met up with some old friends and many new acquaintances – some funny, some eccentric and entertaining, almost all happy to talk about their experiences of past matches on grounds full of character and characters. Not to mention distinguishing characteristics.

It had been a memorable cricketing summer. England had won the World Cup and squared the Ashes series. But the England and Wales Cricket Board still seem bent on pushing the County Championship to the fringes of the season while bringing in yet more gimmicky forms of the game in an attempt to attract big crowds and big money.

All the more reason then why those of us with some feeling for the festive soul of English cricket should continue sampling the pleasures of Scarborough and Arundel, Cheltenham and Chesterfield, for seasons ahead.

For as long as we still can.

On day four Yorkshire beat Nottinghamshire by 143 runs.

The view from the tea-room balcony

Allister Craddock

The distinctive pavilion at North Marine Road from the other side of the ground

Richard Spiller

Boarding houses with vulnerable windows

Richard Spiller

Yorkshire spin wizard Hedley Verity celebrated in the mini-museum

The cricket festival celebrated in the pub up the road

A terrace with a line of washing just beyond one of the scoreboards

Postscript

And so to New Road, Worcester. Yes, I know it's not an outground. Rather it's the headquarters of Worcestershire CCC. But it has the intimacy of a festival setting, with the boundaries close to the spectators. Has character as well, despite the comparatively recent addition of a bog-standard Premier Inn hotel that obscures the view of the nearby bridge over the Severn.

Never the most predictable of rivers, the Severn rose up and flooded both outfield and pitch shortly before near-neighbours and long-time rivals Warwickshire chose to play Essex here in mid-July.

Edgbaston had been required for the World Cup semi-final. The club that I've supported since I was a nipper in south Birmingham could have gone back to the scenic Swan's Nest ground by the Avon in Stratford where they played in the Noughties. Or Coventry and North Warwickshire CC where they'd made regular appearances in the '90s. Or even Rugby School where the county have ventured more recently, albeit for 50-over or Twenty-20 matches.

What those places have in common is that they're within the boundaries of the old county of Warwickshire. Worcester, needless to say, is not.

In the wake of the flood, the Bears ended up having to play the Essex fixture away at what is now the Cloudfm County ground. Used to be known as Chelmsford, in case you're wondering.

I do my best to visit what I should really call Blackfinch New Road at least once a season. Despite local rivalries, I've had a sneaking affection for the place since I first came here as a kid with my cousin Peter Webster whose dad, my Uncle Bert, was Worcester's town clerk.

The likes of Len Coldwell and Jack Flavell would be running into bowl and numbered metal plates would be mounted by hand on to the handsome half-timbered scoreboard. Its remains are still there. I could see its apex peeping over a new-ish stand at the far end of the ground.

Needless to say, the scoreboards today were electronic. And the computers were working overtime soon after I arrived in late morning after a lengthy trek from Foregate Street Station. It was mid-September and day two of the last home game in a season that I didn't want to end. What's more, the visitors were Gloucestershire and I'd been at Cheltenham in the height of summer when Worcs were the visitors.

Another local derby, you might say, with the away side seemingly determined to overtake Worcestershire's first innings total of 221. I'd hardly sat down on a portable plastic seat square of the wicket when the first of three sixes came hurtling in our direction.

Gloucestershire's number nine David Payne, primarily a left-arm medium-fast bowler, was hitting out with just one more wicket to fall. He finished on 43 and his side on 235. More than enough, as it would turn out, with an eventful afternoon to come.

I'd soon fallen into conversation with a bloke called Mike, sporting a cricket sweater and an England cap. He lived in Brighton but, for reasons that were evidently too complicated to explain, he no longer watched Sussex at Hove. Lord's for Middlesex matches had become his home from home. But he had friends he could stay with in Malvern and, like me, loved to come to a game at Worcester once a season.

We were sitting conveniently close to the Ladies' Pavilion, a strategic manoeuvre come the afternoon, bearing in mind that queues for cakes would begin to form long before the tea interval.

First things first, however. When it's lunchtime at Worcester, I traditionally become a man of the Plough – the Plough Inn, that is, one of my top 10 pubs in all England and an easy walk from the ground.

Postscript

Over the Severn Bridge I went at a brisk pace, down the opposite bank for a hundred yards or so and then cut through the grounds of Worcester College. To the left was Glover's Needle, the spire of what was once St Andrew's Church. (It had been clearly visible from the ground, albeit somewhat obscured by that Premier Inn.) To the right was the even more welcome sight of the pub on the corner of ancient Fish Street.

Outside the Plough was a sign proclaiming its abundance of real ales, "local" cider and perry, "plenty of whisky" and "slightly odd conversation". Mainly about cricket on this Tuesday lunchtime, perhaps to the bafflement of the Polish bar-matron who was standing behind eight handpumps at the end of a beautifully tiled passageway and pulling them stalwartly as discerning Worcestershire supporters piled in.

The windowsill and mantelpiece in the room to the left was, as usual, lined with reference books, including a selection of *Wisden's* dating back to the 1940s. And above the mantelpiece was a small glass case framing a bottle of Worcester Sauce. On the bar, meanwhile, were newspapers to borrow – two "broadsheets", *The Guardian* and the *Daily Telegraph*, and one tabloid, the *Worcester News*.

On the other side of the passageway was another room in which the mantelpiece and upper shelves were lined with whisky bottles. "Always around 30 single malts available," said another chalked sign. For now I was quite happy with a pint of Hobson's bitter from across the Shropshire border. It had cost me all of £2.90.

Out on the terrace an abundance of pots and hanging baskets were still in bloom and a "slightly odd" conversation was underway. The subject matter was Sir Frank Worrell who had captained the great West Indian side of 1963 that had first turned me on to Test cricket in the days when I cycled home from school to watch it on my parents' black and white telly. BBC in those days, old chap. Sky was a long way away.

Fascinating though this conversation was, it was interrupted by the wail a fire engine siren on the somewhat congested dual carriageway beyond. As buses and lorries rumbled past, the cathedral tower rose majestically above the hubbub.

And, yes, you could still see it from most parts of the ground. It looked particularly imposing from one of the wooden park benches where I'd parked myself after lunch, near the fabled pear tree. As for the pears, they seemed to be ripening nicely. So did the conkers on the nearby horse chestnut. Well, it was "the season of mists and mellow fruitfulness" I suppose, even if what the cricket writer Stephen Chalke called the Summer's Crown of the County Championship wouldn't be bestowed until the following week – after the Autumn equinox.

Out in the middle the home side were losing wickets at an alarming rate. Not too long after two pm they were 28 for four. I didn't like to break that news to a man in a floppy Worcestershire hat. He was standing under another tree on the far side of the ground, deeply engrossed in what looked like well-worn hardback book. Couldn't help asking him what he was reading, though.

"Aristophanes," he replied.

"So are you a lecturer in ancient Greek playwrights?"

"No, I'm a lawyer. I just like Aristophanes."

I left him to it and walked on, whereupon there was a burst of poetry from the PA system. Well, cleverly contrived rhyming couplets anyway, as a way of telling us that the Ladies' Pavilion was now open for tea and cakes.

Time to skedaddle round the ground and join the queue. It was already stretching down the steps between the benches and was half way back to the main "Graeme Hick Pavilion". Worcestershire, meanwhile, were six wickets down.

"Stands the clock at ten to three

104

Postscript

And is there honey still for tea

With Worcester six for 53?" as the Australian commentator Jim Maxwell might have put it, had he been misquoting the very English Rupert Brooke.

Don't know about honey but there was plenty of jam to slather on sizeable scones when the tables laden with home-made cakes came into view. Eventually. As usual, I had my eye on the coffee cake and, as usual, it was delicious.

Above the table was a banner celebrating "60 years of ladies' pavilion teas". No ladies allowed in the main pavilion back in 1959. But men have been allowed to sit inside or outside this haven of home baking. Except, that is, on any of a short line of fold-up canvas chairs on the terrace at the top of the steps. Those are for "ladies only".

Another sign, by one of the benches where I parked my tray, pointed out that "there will be no teas served on the fourth day". At this rate, there wouldn't be a third day, let alone a fourth. Wickets continued to tumble and in the first over after tea Joe Leach was caught by Miles Hammond off Ryan Higgins, leaving Worcestershire nine down for 90.

Cue a bit of a fight-back, led by Charlie Morris who made an entertaining 29 and helped the home side to 128 before they were all out. By then I was basking in the slowly sinking September sunshine in a stand not far from the main pavilion.

Gloucestershire would go on to win by six wickets the following morning, having been 54 for four by close of play. At least Worcestershire still had the Vitality Blast Twenty-20 finals to look forward to on Saturday. At Edgbaston, as it happened.

For me, though, another season was finally over as I trudged back to the station. Despite the ECB's attempts to give Summer's Crown an autumnal tinge, the words of another man of Warwickshire came to mind. As usual he had the right line and length when he quilled that "summer's lease hath all too short a date".

Worcester old and new, cathedral spire and Premier Inn

Bolthole for a lunchtime pint

The old scoreboard

Reading Aristophanes while wickets tumble

Bibliography

Bird, Dickie: My Autobiography (Hodder and Stoughton, 1997)

Chalke, Stephen: Summer's Crown: The Story of the County Championship. (Fairfield, 2015)

Halford, Brian: The Real Jeeves, the cricketer who gave his life for his country and his name to a legend (Pitch, 2013)

Hamilton, Duncan: A Last English Summer (Quercus, 2010)

Keating, Frank: The Highlights, edited by Matthew Engel (Faber and Faber, 2014)

Kilburn JM: Sweet Summers, edited by Duncan Hamilton (Great Northern, 2008)

Plumptre, George: Homes of Cricket, The First-Class Grounds of England and Wales (Queen Anne Press, 1988)

Simkins, Michael: The Last Flannelled Fool (Ebury Press, 2011)

Also

Arnot, Chris: Britain's Lost Cricket Festivals, the idyllic club grounds that will never again host the world's best players (Aurum, 2014)

and Britain's Lost Cricket Grounds, the hallowed homes of cricket that will never see another ball bowled (Aurum, 2011)

Biography

Chris Arnot was a national freelance feature writer for well over 20 years, writing for *The Guardian*, *The Observer*, *The Independent* and the *Daily Telegraph*. He is also the author of 10 non-fiction books. *Britain's Lost Cricket Festivals* was shortlisted for the Cricket Book of the Year in 2014. *Britain's Lost Cricket Grounds* was acclaimed as "a coffee-table classic for and of posterity" by Frank Keating in *The Guardian* and hailed as "the best sports book of 2011" by Jim Holden in the *Sunday Express*. Chris also wrote *Small Island by Little Train* for the AA and co-wrote *The Archers Archives* for the BBC.